LEADERSHIP BY ATTRACTION

PASS THE PIG

ANNE LAKUSTA
with JEFF LAKUSTA

CONTENTS

FROM THE **AUTHOR**

Dear Leader,

At one point in my life, politics seemed like a good idea. I wanted to improve the world my children would live in, so I became an elected official in our community. After nine years of local service, I saw bigger issues and ran for the state House of Representatives. There were five candidates on voting day and, as one of the top two vote-getters, I entered a runoff election and went to meet the Speaker of the House.

I was excited to show this leader that I was knowledgeable, ready to serve, and ready to learn. Unfortunately, my expectations differed from the Speaker's.

After a cursory greeting, the conversation began.

"Welcome Anne. Please sit down. First I'd like you to sign this pledge card to vote for me as Speaker of the House."

"Excuse me?" I asked.

He slid the paper a bit closer and tapped it twice. "Right here."

I wasn't prepared for this. I was running to have a voice on issues that mattered for my community, and our state. I was ready to discuss that.

So, I replied, "I look forward to discussing issues, and I'm sure I will be happy to support you. But, I don't know enough about you, or the process, to sign a pledge today."

He smiled for a moment, like I'd just fallen into his trap.

"Let me explain. If you do not sign this card immediately, you won't be a very effective representative for your district, even if you are elected. I control committee appointments, and you'll be sitting on the sidelines. I control office space, and you will get none. This is how it works. Your voice is through mine." Tap, tap on the paper one more time. "Right here."

Well, damn! Welcome to politics, I guess? I was beyond stunned. I was angry! He couldn't care less who I was or why I wanted to be there. He shared nothing about his vision or his objectives. He simply declared that, from his position of power, my knowledge, my skills, my passions, my abilities didn't matter at all. I was a tally mark.

"Okay," I answered. "No office? I'll just set up shop on the sidewalk, then. And you can bet I'll invite every news outlet in the state to stop on by for an explanation. We'll see who has a voice!"

That response, it turned out, was bad for my primary election. Sure, I left with my pride, but I also left with a new enemy. The Speaker's political machine focused on my race. In poured money and people, and with all said and done, I lost by forty-seven votes.

The Speaker and I came with different definitions of leadership, and we each left repelled by the other. Attraction could have won me over, but if I'm honest, I did nothing to attract him either. I turned the meeting over and over in my head. What would have made me *want* to support the Speaker? What could have made me clear, eager, and willing to help *his* cause? Where should I have focused to attract his support of my candidacy?

This would have been a great time for Leadership by Attraction by either one of us. Attracting people and results is what creates long lasting teams that accomplish big things, and reach big goals that matter. Instead, an opportunity was missed.

I knew that this idea of attraction was how I intended to lead, but messy, noisy, nasty things kept knocking me off course. These were occasionally momentous, but most often they looked like everyday challenges—an out of control calendar, a miscommunication with a team member, an unexpected roadblock. It wasn't until an only-in-Texas run-in with a pig that I started referring to these obstacles to attraction as "The Pigs."

Each chapter of *Pass the Pig: Leadership by Attraction* introduces a key principle of boosting your attraction alongside a familiar challenge to help you wrestle the pigs.

My leadership roles have ebbed and flowed with life's twists and turns: corporate leadership, entrepreneurship, community activism, politics, investing, volunteering, and motherhood. And most recently, being called upon to lead remotely and using virtual tools that were new to me. I've called ten different places home, won and lost elections, owned and sold multiple businesses, survived cancer, coached leaders and worn many hats, often at the same time. Frequently, choosing to lead meant working through the unanticipated, the unplanned and the unknown.

Through my journey of life and leadership, I have moved constantly through Robert Kiyosaki's four quadrants—Employee, Self-Employed, Business Owner, Investor—every step bringing opportunities to lead people who desire to make their own impact.

To me, hierarchy has always been a complete turnoff when others relied on it. I wanted to see "You have to" transformed into "I want to," for both myself and those around me. As remote work is embraced more broadly, that transformation is more important today than ever before.

Being at the top of the ladder may sound good, but don't you want more than one ladder? And maybe a few side journeys along the way? I think that "Don't settle" means not settling for just one rung on one ladder, even if it's at the top.

I've worked with and for great leaders, terrible leaders, and a bunch of mediocre, well-intentioned leaders… and I've been great, terrible, and mediocre too.

Leadership is a journey, not a destination, just like life is more than climbing the next rung of some ladder. Here are some highlights along my own path:

- As a politician and president of a school district with forty thousand kids, five thousand teachers, and a one-hundred-million-dollar budget, I found consensus to build a team from individual leaders.

- As a corporate leader, I incorporated the individual visions of more than four hundred entrepreneurs each recruited to pay eighteen thousand dollars a year for leadership, education, tools and support.

- As a broker for over nine billion dollars in sales volume, I led four thousand real estate agent entrepreneurs.

- As a volunteer and advisory board member for a nonprofit, I shaped the shared passion of strangers to see what could be, rather than what was, in order to raise over four million dollars.

- As a corporate leadership coach, I discovered that money rarely motivates people to be their best.

- As a cancer survivor, I needed leadership from doctors, surgeons, friends, and family members, and during the eighteen months of treatments, I learned the power of accepting help, modeling strength, striving to give hope to others, and expressing endless gratitude.

Leadership shows up again and again, in all facets of life. No matter the role, if I didn't have influence, I didn't have anything. Even (or especially!) as a mom, I could make all the rules I wanted—but if no one else wanted to be at practice on time, we were late.

Leadership by Attraction is a highly adaptable set of principles that helps you analyze your team, your project, and your leadership to attract your people and your results. You can't attract everything and everyone, but you can attract more. These principles and exercises will increase your influence when and where you need it most.

Put Leadership by Attraction into action, and watch as attraction works in your favor.

It's all about the journey.
See you there,

Anne

WHAT IS **LEADERSHIP BY ATTRACTION?**

Forcing people and results is less effective than attracting them. To really understand Leadership by Attraction, we need to dig into its two main components, leadership and attraction.

WHAT IS LEADERSHIP?

Leadership as a concept can be hard to decipher because its many definitions often conflict with each other. Dictionaries use words like *directing, controlling, governing, captaining,* and *supervising.* Articles talk about *motivating, inspiring, guiding, strategizing,* and so on. The difference in strategies is stark, but leadership's goal remains the same: achieve results with people.

If leadership is linked to results and people, what's with the competing definitions? The answer lies in how leadership has changed as work increasingly depends on *individual* needs, wants, and demands.

Historically, leadership was management. It was task-, process-, and system-oriented; get the process ironed out, and success would follow. But, as Greek philosopher Heraclitus said, "The only constant in life is change," and it is oh so true in the world of work. Today, managing tasks and systems no longer equals success. Leaders may try direct-and-control, but the tasks are changing and processes move too quickly for leaders to have all the answers all the time.

When the United States government first tracked work hours in the late 1800s, people worked one hundred hours each week.[1] That certainly gives perspective on why the introduction of the eight-hour, nine-to-five workday was considered good for all workers—indeed, good for everyone.

Can you imagine any policy or practice that would be considered good for everyone today? Take work-from-home policies for example, which were thrown into the limelight by the sudden office closures forced by COVID-19. Some allowed employees to work when convenient for them, while others immediately installed website blockers, enforced limits on scheduled breaks, and launched timecards. We can't agree on which benefits best accommodate health concerns, minimum wage, or even how much paid time off is appropriate. Leaders now need to coordinate people across an ever-expanding variety of systems, many of which compete with the old nine-to-five paradigm. Here are a few examples:

- **Part-Time Work:** Between 1990 and 2019, the percentage of workers working part time (35 hours or less, 16 years or older) at their primary job has risen by 38%.[2]

---

1 Ward, Marguerite. "A brief history of the 8-hour workday, which changed how Americans work." CNBC. Accessed: August 2020. https://www.cnbc.com/2017/05/03/how-the-8-hour-workday-changed-how-americans-work.html

2 Duffin, Erin. Number of part-time employees in the United States from 1990 to 2019. Statista. Bureau of Labor Statistics. Accessed: August 2020. https://www.statista.com/statistics/192338/number-of-part-time-employees-in-the-us-since-1990/

- **Remote Work:** Pre-Covid, Gallup was already reporting that the number of employees working remotely at least part of the time had risen to 43%.[3] As the tools available to us continue to improve, projections show this number increasing long term.

- **On-Demand Work:** The on-demand or gig economy, the temporary labor force, freelancing, side hustles… no matter what you call it, technology has rapidly expanded options to generate income. Gallup reports that more than three and a half million people worked at on-demand jobs in 2016, a number forecasted to triple by 2021.[4]

- **Flexible Work:** A fixed income at a single company location is no longer necessary, and individuals increasingly view it as incompatible to their lives and schedules. The Australian Fair Work Commission, for example, proposed a federal employment law requiring employers to seriously consider approving formal, flexible working arrangements.

These arrangements not only create more possibilities than ever before, but also intensify a sense of individualism at work. Leaders must navigate not only changing ways of doing work, but also changing expectations of how we work together.

LEADERSHIP IS DEFINITELY NOT…

Having people report to you. *Getting help* is often the best way to move forward, and yet *having* help does not make someone a leader. Getting

---

3 Gallup. 2017 "State of the American Workplace by Gallup" Accessed: August 2020. file:///C:/Users/Anne/Downloads/Gallup_State_of_the_American_Workplace_Report.pdf

4 Gallup. 2017 "State of the American Workplace by Gallup" Accessed: August 2020. file:///C:/Users/Anne/Downloads/Gallup_State_of_the_American_Workplace_Report.pdf

help to avoid the pain of crushing workloads is self-preservation. Getting help to accomplish a task is a way to keep the business running.

Companies that appear successful may operate on the principle of hiring help for self-preservation or keeping the lights on. They're buying hours from hands. The hands may be skilled, or not, but either way they are a tool for completing a task. Just like any tool, they accomplish the task and nothing more. Hired help punches in and punches out both physically and mentally. Directing hired help is a remnant of old-school leadership, fitting better today into the idea of management rather than leadership. After all, when you receive a service from someone hired to perform a task and nothing more, you know it—and usually, you don't like it. The same is true for a leader who is just doing a task and probably wishing they were anywhere else!

A job title. Having a position doesn't make you a leader. Leadership is not about kings and serfs, bosses and employees, command and control, managers and a production line. It cannot only be about a position of formal authority. Whether you have a title or not, *you* have the opportunity to be a leader.

Compliance. Organizations have things that must get done. So, they develop policies, procedures, and rules designed to force people to do what the organization needs. In many organizations, compliance itself is the target—the optimal outcome. But, while compliance is necessary at times, it is not leadership.

Let's be honest. Nobody works to work. Employees care about company or group success only as a vessel for their own. When the two align, that's attraction. Even Fortune 500 CEOs are driven not by detached company success, but by *their* own aspirations, dreams for what *their* lives could look like, and what incentives provide a means to *their* ends. CEOs leverage the company to achieve their own fulfillment. Those who are most successful help many others (employees, partners, investors, etc.) achieve the same along the way.

Still, "Because I said so" and "Because it's your job" linger. Too frequently top-down leaders are presumptuous, saying, "I've been successful, so do what I say, when I say it, how I say it." Sometimes leaders may seem to be confident, but then they fail to believe in themselves enough to offer genuine opportunities to others.

People no longer believe a title gives someone the right to pontificate from their corner office. No one aspires to be *that* leader. No one automatically trusts *that* leader, either, and certainly no one chooses to follow *that* leader. People want to give their best to a leader that cares about their success, a leader that can help them be successful, a leader that will provide stepping stones to bigger achievements. Influence today must be earned, and influence is attraction. Leaders are only as successful as the people they attract.

WHAT IS ATTRACTION?

It is interest, energy, and enthusiasm from others to help attain results. You attract people *because* you have an impact on their families and futures. Attraction in careers, dreams, and families is not entertainment. It's a high-stakes effort that requires rebalancing, intentionality, and focus.

Since the antonyms for attraction are *disinterest, apathy, revulsion,* and *repulsion,* it's important to understand what it is not.

ATTRACTION IS DEFINITELY NOT...

Being a "born leader." You do not have to be the most charismatic, the sexiest, or the best at anything. Instead, leaders who attract must constantly learn, evolve, adapt, and change. They listen and ask for help, or they fail. Sure, some find public speaking, or remembering names, or making flashy presentations easier than others... but such skills alone do not drive attraction.

Being a celebrity. Celebrities can be leaders, and leaders can be celebrities. In a loud world though, being the loudest can create an illusion of leadership; social media influencers, for example, can sometimes change people's actions or purchasing decisions. However, a celebrity's importance to your life is lessened by distance. You're a voyeur, watching these people from afar for entertainment. Their problems and goals don't affect your family or your future. You choose whether to tune in or disconnect. People turn on celebrities in a heartbeat. One wrong tweet or paparazzi picture can change the relationship completely. That *distance* reduces the probability of developing sustainable attraction.

Being the best. Being skilled in a certain area or task does not mean that people will be influenced by you, support you, follow you. I know some believe, "Well, others should follow me because I'm awesome at _____." But the world is overflowing with people who are good at something, and it is starved for people who can work with others, let alone lead them. As a leader, you want to be the best in attracting the right people. Steve Jobs said, "Go after the cream of the cream. A small team of A+ players can run circles around a giant team of B and C players." Basketball great Michael Jordan says it this way: "Talent wins games, but teamwork and intelligence win championships."

SO WHAT IS LEADERSHIP BY ATTRACTION?

We all want to be a part of the story. We want to engage. We want our time, energy, and resources to be inspired, not drained. We reject days spent toiling. We want to be motivated, inspired, and yes... happy.

We want to be attracted, and so we follow those who create attraction. That is marketing, that is technology, and that is leadership.

The average tenure of companies on the S&P 500 is shrinking. More than fifty percent of the companies on the list are expected to be replaced over the next ten years.[5] Disruption, innovation, and fast-paced change are a fact. Attracting the right people is imperative for success, no matter how big or small the project may be. Whether they're building a new corporate vision, planting a tomato garden, or structuring a major bond initiative, leaders need advice, ideas, support, and experts.

Attracting your people demands that you know what you really want. It requires a decisive statement of your goals and dreams. Deciding what you really want, and why, may be the biggest hurdle, because without that conviction, there can be no Leadership by Attraction.

ATTRACT YOUR PEOPLE AND YOUR RESULTS

People have more options and more control over what happens in their daily life. Our society values self-actualization, meaningful answers to "Why am I doing this?" But how does a business owner, a coach, a politician, an entrepreneur, a CEO, or a parent accommodate everyone's individual pursuit of purpose?

Leadership by Attraction embraces the reality that people work for their own dreams and are increasingly likely to pursue them elsewhere if necessary. In writing this book, I spoke with great leaders and studied the science of leadership, achievement and results. It turns out that successful leaders have always leveraged attraction. It's always been a sign of good leadership. What's changed, is that today it is no longer optional. Today, you must intentionally leverage attraction. Leading

---

5 "Digital Transformation is Racing Ahead and No Industry Is Immune." Harvard Business Review. Accessed: August 2020. https://hbr.org/sponsored/2017/07/digital-transformation-is-racing-ahead-and-no-industry-is-immune-2

people who can walk away at any time is almost magical—and today it is a leader's reality.

Leadership by Attraction will not help you attract everyone, but it will help attract your people. It does not churn out a certain type of leader, because complexity, disruption, and change mean there is no one "right" way to lead anyway.

Leadership by Attraction helps leaders of all types attract the talent and the results they desire with five principles:

- Make It Clear
- Make It Fun
- Make It Yours
- Make It Theirs
- Make It Happen

These principles show what you need people to give in order to get what you want. And they show the inverse: what you need to give so those around you get what they want too. Leadership by Attraction is about attracting people, yes, but perhaps most importantly, it is about attracting focus, energy, momentum, and achievement.

This book is not an academic dissertation. It facilitates and demands action. Part 1 explores the five principles, through science and experiences that bring each to life. Part 2 makes it personal, assessing your progress and pointing to action where it matters most.

Look at your project, your organization, and your day-to-day. Join me on your journey as you begin something new or refresh something old. Find your Leadership by Attraction as both you, and the world, keep changing.

PART 01

LEADERSHIP
BY ATTRACTION

MAKE IT **CLEAR**

I went from selling houses on my own to leading two hundred people overnight. Suddenly, Realtors who'd created businesses much larger than mine were under my leadership, and so were others who were brand new. I was confident in my ability as a Realtor but unsure whether I could matter to everyone. And the areas in need of my time and energy felt limitless.

I entered my first week unclear about who I was in this new context, where we were going, and what I expected. And then my phone began to ring because business doesn't stop when you're unclear.

"When you know what matters most, everything makes sense. When you don't know what matters most, anything makes sense."

— GARY KELLER, *The One Thing*

"I am so going to sue you," a woman said over competing background noise. "You're in big trouble. I just showed a home, and when I opened the door a pig literally attacked us."

"Oh." I replied, suddenly recognizing the background noise.

"It's still chasing us. Grab him!" she shouted at someone off the phone. "It's chasing my buyer's toddler around the front yard. And... oh, there it goes, it's running down the street now. I hope it gets run over."

"I'm on it," I said, and called the listing agent, who now apparently worked for me, to explain that a pig had chased a baby and was now loose in the neighborhood.

"That's a fifty-thousand-dollar prize hog!" said the Realtor.

"Then I guess you'd better go get it."

Over the next several days, my life was absorbed by this pig. The potential buyer was traumatized by the toddler's run-in, the homeowner was livid that their prized hog had nearly escaped, and the showing service was upset that the showing had gone so wrong. It was a ridiculous mess.

This was not an attractive start to my new job, and my failure in leadership was a total lack of clarity.

FOCUSING FACTS

- Around 50% of employees don't know what's expected of them at work.[6]
- Only 49% of full-time employees have "a great deal of trust" in those working above and alongside them.[7]
- 89% of bosses believe that people quit because they want more money. Only 12% of people actually quit because they want more money.[8]

WHAT IS CLARITY?

It's tempting to think that a lack of clarity results in chaos, but it's usually just an epic slowdown in activity and progress. You're paralyzed,

---

6 Rigoni, Brandon, and Nelson, Bailey. "Do Employees Really Know What's Expected of Them?" Gallup. Accessed: August 2020. https://news.gallup.com/businessjournal/195803/employees-really-know-expected.aspx

7 Twaronite, Karen. "A Global Survey on the Ambiguous State of Employee Trust." Harvard Business Review. Accessed: August 2020. https://hbr.org/2016/07/a-global-survey-on-the-ambiguous-state-of-employee-trust

8 Sturt, David, and Nordstrom, Todd. "10 Shocking Workplace Stats You Need To Know." Forbes. Accessed: August 2020. https://www.forbes.com/sites/davidsturt/2018/03/08/10-shocking-workplace-stats-you-need-to-know

and you stagnate. Clarity attracts by establishing trusting relationships between you and the people around you.

Without clarity, the brain responds emotionally and sometimes illogically. Psychologists call these moments "ambiguous decisions." They are very different than risky decisions. A risky decision involves a lack of directional certainty ("I think it will go like this, but I'm not sure"). An ambiguous decision involves a total lack of direction ("I have no idea how, or where, this will go").

Ambiguous decisions—with no clarity—activate a part of the brain called the amygdala.[9] While the right brain is known for controlling creativity and the left brain is known for controlling mathematical skills and hand-eye coordination, the amygdala is best known for its role in controlling emotion, fear and how they impact decision making. The amygdala stores memories and is involved in how or why we experience anxiety.

A lack of clarity eliminates the ability to clearly identify threats, which causes us to feel fear, and, whether consciously or subconsciously, that fear causes us to slow down. We become paralyzed, not chaotic.

With clarity, we make decisions without fear. There are plenty of examples of leaders deciding to Make It Clear. Salesforce's Marc Benioff made it clear that trust is a higher priority than company growth.[10] Netflix's Reed Hastings made it clear that employee freedom comes with the expectation of results.[11] Both of these leaders, and many others, have used that clarity to attract.

---

9   Hsu, Ming; Bhatt, Meghana; Adolphs, Ralph; Tranel, Daniel; Camerer, Colin F. "Neural Systems Responding to Degrees of Uncertainty in Human Decision-Making." Science. 09 Dec 2005: Vol. 310, Issue 5754, pp. 1680-1683.

10   Winfrey, Graham. "4 Leadership Strategies Marc Benioff Swears By." Accessed: August 2020. https://www.inc.com/graham-winfrey/marc-benioff-salesforce-ceo-leadership-lessons-facebook.html

11   Snyder, Bill. "Netflix Founder Reed Hastings: Make as Few Decisions as Possible." Accessed: August 2020. https://www.gsb.stanford.edu/insights/netflix-founder-reed-hastings-make-few-decisions-possible

WANTED

THE PING-PONG PIG

- Hangs around those who say,
  - ▷ "I can't do one more thing!"
  - ▷ "I'm working as hard as I can!"
  - ▷ "I need my to-do list!"

- Crimes:
  - ▷ Distracting from what matters
  - ▷ Masquerading as important
  - ▷ Squealing for attention

Ping-Pong Pig's a nasty one, wanted for hogging attention. It's a real sneaky character, with a million disguises. This pig always seems the loudest and most pressing, but it'll eat your time and energy without ever helping you get ahead.

Society encourages busyness. But busyness tends to produce a sense of being tired and overwhelmed rather than results. Clarity's most tenacious pig is not taking it easy. It's busyness without intentional advancement toward a goal.

Ping-Pong Pig is indiscriminate activity, the endless bouncing from task to task. You know the feeling. You lose control, so your days fill with tasks and activities but not progress. Marking things off of a to-do list can feel productive—that shot of dopamine—but there's a trap. It's too easy to stay mindlessly busy rather than taking selective action on things that matter and that yield the results that you want the most. Ping-Pong Pig squeals loudly in your ear, pushing you to be busy with what you may want or need *right now,* not what you want *the very most!* Ping-Pong Pig is just rolling in the mud of what feels like a necessity. But immediate gratification doesn't get you closer to the bigger goals.

Busyness can be a form of laziness. That fact makes busy people mad, because being busy feels so productive! Busyness is a necessity, not a choice, after all. Pausing to analyze whether that busyness is really useful would be a waste, right? But being sloppy with your time is a definite pig. Analyze your time, and you may find that most of it is spent worrying about being busy, feeling burdened by being busy, or thinking about being busy. Being overwhelmed has become an identity. Everyone has the same amount of time each day. Spend it on bigger vision and bigger goals.

Ping-Pong Pig is not attractive. You may get stuff done, but who wants to share that journey? It looks exhausting, unclear, and not at all desirable as a way of living. Turn Ping-Pong Pig's catchphrases, like "I'm working as hard as I can," from points of pride into red flags: you've got to pass this pig.

When the urgent and necessary overtake the strategic and intentional, Ping-Pong Pig's at your door!

WHY CLARITY ATTRACTS

When you lead, lots of things are unclear. Leaders execute current plans while focusing on future opportunity; they make difficult decisions with money; they cut through fuzzy, moving targets to set goals; and they work with people who are, well, people. Ambiguity comes with the territory, and yet it is a leader's job to make certain things clear.

Clarity is a decision, not a natural outcome, because there's always some question unanswered, some stone unturned. When you Make It Clear, you decide to remove white space, cut through clutter, and simplify the world around you. When you decide to be clear, it is in spite of everything else.

- **Clarity empowers.** If "Performance = Potential – Interference," then clarity is what removes the interference. Clarity is momentum with reduced resistance. We know what to do next to keep things flowing.

- **Clarity focuses.** It replaces distraction with confidence in what's most important. After all, it's easy to avoid important things by being too busy with unimportant things.

- **Clarity accelerates.** It speeds up discussions and decisions, and it clears a path to results.

- **Clarity is kind.** Direct conversations may make you uncomfortable, but indirect, unreal, and un-had conversations are unkind. Clarity creates trust, sets realistic expectations, and decreases stress.

CLARITY IS KIND

Whether the company where a friend worked was downsizing, it was the worst-kept secret. Everyone knew it was coming but not when or how. So, the months dragged with secret meetings and growing anxiety.

My friend was notified that in this reorganization he would be promoted. Part of that new position would be notifying people of layoffs. Now, he had to tell people he'd known for years that they were being let go.

He planned a meeting and prepared his talking points. At first he planned an elaborate defense of the company, explaining why layoffs were necessary. But before making that mistake, he considered what he'd want to know. He could handle, would *want*, honest straightforwardness: "You're being let go on this day and the company is offering services to help."

The conversation was challenging, but he was shocked that some people thanked him for finally telling it like it is. By sharing a concrete timeline and plan, he had ended their angst and worry.

Clarity is kindness.

Don't get in the way of your own success by lacking the courage and forethought to have tough conversations. No one succeeds without them.

WHERE CLARITY ATTRACTS

Getting clarity right means removing distractions, lowering barriers, and eliminating conversations or tasks that aren't important. It also means creating autonomy for your people because *their* clarity gives them confidence.

Getting clarity wrong, whether too much or too little, can repel others. Yes, that's right. Miss on clarity, allow uncertainties to creep in, and you'll push your people and your results further away. So, let's look at the two most important areas in which to achieve clarity: who you are and where you're going. Plan to revisit them frequently along your journey.

REPELLENT: TOO MUCH CLARITY

Supervision may be part of leadership, but when does it become micromanagement?

Curiosity and a willingness to learn are keys to avoiding repelling people through micromanagement. No one sets out to be a micromanager, but as your experience grows, micromanagement can creep in. Experience heightens your ability to spot negative outcomes, and it's tempting to provide constant "help" to avoid them.

Research shows that micromanagement—that is, providing too much clarity—detracts from the quality of work output,[12] lowers morale, and ultimately makes people quit.[13]

Which negative outcomes are critical to avoid? Be willing to provide freedom in lower risk areas as your trust in your team grows. You'll either be surprised that there was "another way," or the other person will gain some experience and their own ability to spot negative outcomes will increase.

Not convinced? See if your clarity is actually coming from stubbornness. When is the last time you learned something new or asked for suggestions? If others aren't occasionally changing how you think and you are not putting what you learn into action, you may be digging your heels in for no real reason. Encourage input, and give feedback/ideas without instruction.

You want to be strong and learning-based, not arrogant and immovable. So, be persistent about achieving a result, but not immovable on the strategies to get there.

---

12 DeCaro, M. S., Thomas, R. D., Albert, N. B., & Beilock, S. L. (2011). Choking under pressure: Multiple routes to skill failure. Journal of Experimental Psychology: General, 140(3), 390-406.

13 Collins, Sandra K., and Collins, Kevin S. (2002). Micromanagement—a costly management style. Radiology Management, 24(6), 32-35.

WHO YOU ARE

Who are you? Do you know? People avoid leaders who are unclear on who they are, and vague leadership yields vague results. Ambiguity about you as an individual and as a leader spills into the whole organization, team, or project.

It's all too easy to watch this play out in public. Leaders attempt to repair lapses in clarity on who they are with well-planned, public apologies. It seems that every day another celebrity or executive is apologizing for some personal behavior gone wrong. Then the crisis management wheels start turning, and the whole misstep becomes painful and costly.

Clarity on Who You Are incorporates your values, your capabilities, and your first response.

YOUR VALUES

I hesitated to use the word *values* because over time it has become politically charged. In this case, I simply mean what you value.

What's most important to you can be a powerful magnet. Reflecting these core values in your work and daily life is powerful in today's increasingly fuzzy world. It's not about being perfect. Make mistakes and face unexpected challenges head on, reacting along the same principles you use in day-to-day decisions. Lead with your values and showcase them by making them visible in everything you do.

My husband and I are alumni of Wake Forest University and recently were part of a pilot movement called A Call to Conversation. The now-national program connects strangers for intimate conversation on rarely discussed, thought-provoking topics. Our random group was challenged to discuss the word *character*. Can you teach character? Can you recruit character? And what's a leader's role as it relates to character? It was a fascinating conversation, fueled by the participants' varied backgrounds and perspectives. After a night of lively debate, the table agreed that yes, you can teach it, you can recruit it, and we should insist on it in ourselves and in those who affect our lives. A Call to Conversation attracted us again to our university and to those who make up its community. Wake Forest's motto is Pro Humanitate (For Humanity), and that evening we found it with renewed clarity.

Be cautious when considering "company values." A list of company values on a poster feels empty when the leaders do not embrace them fully. When those supposed values are absent in the company's day-to-day, that poster will attract only graffiti and sad humor. Consider, for example, the highly visible values of Enron: "Communication, Respect, Integrity, and Excellence." Leadership by Attraction helps *leaders,* not companies, attract people and results that reflect *their* values.

Make your company values clear, visible, and supported, by starting with *your* leadership. Boost *your* attraction by providing the people around you with clarity on *your* values. Hire those whose values align with yours, and coach the leaders around and with you so that company values are a part of daily life at your organization—not just a sign on the wall.

Immediate relationships are where clarity about what's important to you matters most: your boss, your colleagues, and those you see frequently. Look for the values you share. The greater your impact on their time, their financial future, and their family lives, the more likely it is that one breach or lapse in clarity on who you are will create uncertainty and weaken trust. If your lack of strength or consistency harms their journey, your lack of clarity becomes a serious repellent.

YOUR CAPABILITIES

Who you are is also reflected in your confidence and competence. Are your skills strong enough to lead in this area? Do you have the connections to get the information you need? Will you ask for help when you need it? Will you be honest when communicating progress and failures—and your contribution to either? Are you confident enough to be humble and grateful?

Knowing and living your capabilities is critical to being clear on who you are. It shows up as confidence, which fuels energy and belief in your ability to handle the day's challenges. A leader's confidence supercharges the team. For example, confident leaders radiate the ability to make good decisions and reassure the team that time and talent is being spent productively.

Not good at something important? Assess whether you personally need to learn it or should attract someone else with that talent instead. Clarity in your capabilities strengthens your team. Unclear leaders are too insecure to admit that there may be a better way to get something done. Succeed by attracting the best people for the job, not by always attempting to be the best person for the job. Consider the famous quote by Confucius: "If you are the smartest person in the room, you are in the wrong room."

YOUR FIRST RESPONSE

Nobody likes to be surprised by their leader, not about things that matter. Consistent and predictable responses move things along. If you can predict what your boss is going to do, you don't have to spend as much energy managing that relationship, planning interactions, dealing with interference or questioning, or justifying actions. Stable expectations free people to do their jobs and be creative within that framework. They experience more freedom while accomplishing what's needed.

A predictable first response helps the team prepare:

- Miss quota? Will the leader talk to you personally or call you out publicly, thinking it's funny?
- Have a new idea? Does the leader love new ideas or change slowly?
- Want to do something? Does the leader prefer details or a summary?

Leadership is the heartbeat of the organization. If the beat is irregular, the organization has problems. Clarity in your first response gives your team a sense of safety, stability, and security. When a person's heartbeat is irregular, they may need a pacemaker to "shock" the heart back into a regular beat. If an organization's heartbeat is irregular, external or internal challenges may shock things back to clarity and consistency. Within a clear and predictable framework, more bold, creative, and game-changing things can occur.

Don't confuse stubbornness with clarity. When given new information, strong people develop and evolve their opinions. Your life (not to mention someone else's career) stagnates when you're wrong and don't admit it. Some leaders fool themselves into thinking that stubbornness is tough-mindedness, when in fact, being obstinate is frequently just selfishness or laziness. Creating clarity around your values, capabilities, and first response fosters consistent expectations, a productive rhythm, and a continuous desire to learn.

WHERE YOU'RE GOING

What's your destination? Lack of clarity around where you are going leads to frustration, not autonomy. If people's days are filled with directionless tasks, you're all likely heading for tiredness, frustration, and burnout rather than accomplishment.

Coca Cola's mission statement of "Refresh the world" has allowed them to stay true to their core business, while expanding and innovating and changing through the years. Bill Gates's vision of "A computer on every desk and in every home" provided clarity without listing the exact steps to get there. That allowed for innovation and change along the way.

You may not have exact clarity on what needs to be done by when. That's fine! Attracting the right people will help generate the steps needed to get results. So, instead of worrying about clarifying exactly what needs to be done, be clear on where you're going.

If I ate lettuce and immediately saw the scale drop one pound, I would eat more lettuce. If I made two phone calls and landed a new deal, I'd make more phone calls. It's the time, space, and energy between doing a task and seeing the results that's frustrating. Being reminded of the big vision over and over again encourages focus. Leaders need to provide constant reminders of how each day—today—contributes to a larger success story.

I love Aristotle's "Quality is not an act, but a habit." You can't expect quality without clarity on what that is. Quality can be inspired by your end goal, even when the specifics for each step have not yet been laid out.

Big-rig trucks on the highway are plastered with reminders of a larger story: "Helping people keep their promises" or "Creating memories one delivery at a time." That's much more than one driver on one road. If those values are also a part of day-to-day operations, I can see those big visions actually motivating the driver as well as the CEO.

Ambiguity about where you're going is a decelerator. Confused teams get distracted by low-priority work or have members duplicating efforts. In an effort to find clarity, confused teams trade endless streams of emails, texts, and phone calls, bogging down their days with unproductive moments. Confusion fuels squabbles because no one is sure who has the authority to make a decision. Things fall through the cracks because no one is sure who is responsible for the crack. When people know where they're going—and feel empowered to get there— things keep moving ahead.

Finding and living clarity on who you are and where you're going will keep you and your team on the path to success, even when that path inevitably zigzags. As challenges and changes enter your world, let clarity accelerate your progress and give power to your leadership.

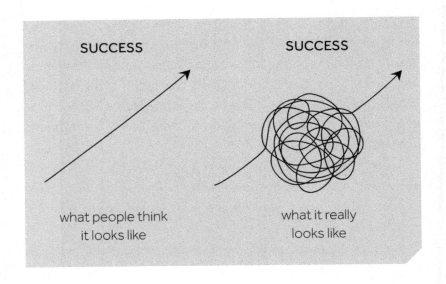

SUCCESS

SUCCESS

what people think
it looks like

what it really
looks like

KNOW WHERE YOU ARE

Both leaders and their team members must be clear in the two most attractive areas—who you are and where you're going.

On any given subject there are four potential communication outcomes: paralysis when *everyone's* unclear, a communication problem when *they're* unclear, a perception problem when *you're* unclear, and attractive clarity where *everyone* is *clear*. Attractive clarity is what you're after.

The following framework provides action steps for these states of clarity. New project? New role? New company? Feeling stagnant? Feeling overwhelmed? Try it out to see how clear things are and how clarity might help attract the right people and right results.

PARALYSIS PROBLEM

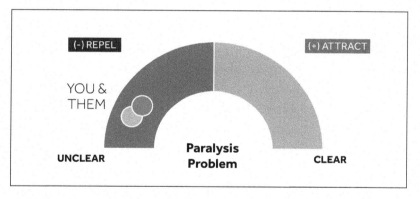

When you are unclear and they are unclear, action is slow or nonexistent. It's the worst place to be, and yet it's not uncommon. Sometimes new jobs and projects are unclear because no one took the time to define or even learn about what's most important. Other times it's the old jobs and projects that are unclear because what's most important got lost over the months or years, or perhaps what's most important has changed. Whether the project is truly at a standstill or just feels like it's stuck in quicksand, awareness of the paralysis problem is the most important step. Get out by asking more questions. Listen intently, and your clarity of the obstacles and options will increase.

COMMUNICATION PROBLEM

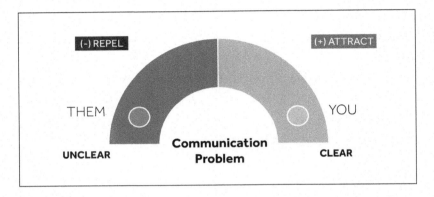

If you're clear and they're not, a lack of communication is probably to blame. It may be that others aren't comfortable asking you clarifying questions to cut through ambiguity. It may be that they feel overwhelmed by the big vision and unclear on the next step. Or, it may be that they don't feel they're getting through to you. Have they been allowed to disagree? Have they been allowed to share a lack of confidence in a skill they believe is necessary? Has communication been very open and honest? Do you need to repeat or demonstrate or communicate in a different way? If they lack clarity in their understanding or strength in their commitment, further communication is the best solution.

PERCEPTION PROBLEM

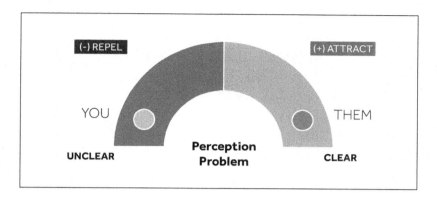

You have a perception problem with they think they know who you are and where you're going, but you're actually uncertain. Think of a time when you internalized your uncertainty. Those around you thought they clearly knew your goals and capabilities, but you still had questions or concerns that you kept to yourself. Maybe you put on a good front, or maybe change happened so abruptly that you hadn't yet adapted.

Maybe you thought, "Fake it till you make it." Things function under this cover-up while everything changes: you take a new role, your role requirements change, you work with a new leader, or you face personal challenges.

The size of a perception problem may relate to how well people know you. Your inner circle may be aware of your lack of clarity, while those farther away read your actions as having clarity.

Common clarity detractors include:

- Distractions: Personal challenges, health problems, just having a bad day
- Uncertainty about capabilities: Uneasiness about own skills
- Noise: News, Gossip, Happenings outside of your control

- Mismatched priorities: Competing objectives that don't seem to compute

Imitating confidence, competence, and an optimistic mindset is risky. You can keep up the charade, but only for so long. Remember, you don't need clarity on everything. Get yourself clear first, and then make perception match reality.

ATTRACTIVE CLARITY

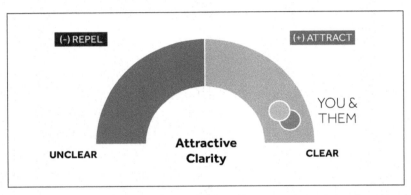

Attractive clarity is the magic spot where everyone is on the same page. Who you are, where you're going, and what's expected are aligned. Trust is high, and all barriers within your control have been removed—it's time to execute. Attractive clarity makes other people look at your team, business, or project with envy because it's surprisingly rare. As a leader, you might experience envy as a form of attraction as you see a spike in job applications, phone calls, or attention to what you're doing.

You want to operate here 100% of the time. When everyone is clear on who you are and where you're going, you attract the right people and produce the right results.

How could I have achieved and maintained attractive clarity when the pig entered the picture? Well, I could have passed the pig.

PASS THE PIG

I needed to know about "the pig incident," but there should have never been an expectation that I'd solve it. As the new leader of almost two hundred people, I needed to focus on improving their lives, not chasing a pig.

When it comes time to Make It Clear, every leader meets a few pigs: challenges that seem to need your attention. If you take the pig, your team is thrilled. They don't want to deal with something that far outside the framework—and yet it's still part of their job, not yours. How can you say no so that your team knows they need to take the pig back? Leadership by Attraction creates an environment where your team will keep the pig in the first place because they *want* you to spend time on other things!

Over the years, I took this story to heart and told the Realtors who worked for me why I had to pass the pig. But only in Texas would it happen again! Years later, yet another property turned out to have undisclosed swine, but this time around, an agent texted me a video of them carrying the seventy-five pound pig out before the showing. No problem, no action required, just a smiley emoji and a great story!

MY BELOVED TO-DO LIST

One day I was meeting my coach with the yellow pad containing my to-do list open on my desk between us.

"Oh, what's that?" my coach asked.

"Today's list," I said. I flipped through three pages of things that needed to get done, showing off how much I planned to achieve. I was successful, the office was growing, and people liked working for me. These weekly coaching sessions helped me find ways to get better.

"Wow, you have a lot of things to do," my coach said. "Why don't we just pick the most important things? Maybe that's something I can help you with today."

"Oh yes," I answered. "I do feel overwhelmed many days. That would be wonderful."

My coach found a separate pad of paper and said, "Let's make a separate list. Just tell me what your three or four most important things are, and I'll write them down."

I thought and whittled things down as my coach scribbled on a separate pad.

"Awesome!" he said. "Let's compare. Can I see your to-do list, and I'll hold it next to mine?"

As soon as I handed it to him, he walked out of my office to the parking lot, where he locked my list in the trunk of his car.

"Well great!" I sneered, infuriated. "I hope you're proud of yourself. Now I'll just let down everyone on that pad. No way I'll remember all that." I spent several minutes venting. "I wasn't hired to let people down. But ha ha! You're so funny. It's hilarious to disappoint people!"

"Okay," he said when I took a breath. "I'll make you a deal. If you still want your to-do list back two weeks from now, I'll bring it back with interest—a gift card wherever you want. But, if you don't want it, you have to be honest and call me, because I don't want to drive up here."

"Great! I'll make that deal all day long. I want a Nordstrom gift card. I'm all about it! And I hope it's a pain in your ass to bring it back."

Two weeks later I made the call. "I don't know what was on that pad," I said, "and I don't think I care." I got my important things done, and I have no clue what happened to everything else. They didn't matter.

Love checking off items on your list? If so, you've put a ceiling on how much you can achieve. Do you think most successful leaders end everyday with everything done? Of course not. It's impossible. I needed to learn to lead through others, and trust systems and processes. I needed to learn to go to bed with things undone and unresolved, knowing that tomorrow would bring resolutions to some issues and new challenges, too. I couldn't let my leadership be limited by my to-do list.

START ATTRACTING

When everyone is clear on who you are and where you're going, you attract the right people and the right results. Now you just have to maintain by attracting the right work and repelling the wrong work. Passing the pig is a fun way to remember to repel the wrong work. Why did the pig come your way at all? There must be a gap in clarity on your skillsets or priorities.

If you want to assess where you are and maximize Clarity's most attractive characteristics, look ahead to Part 2 of this book.

FIND YOUR PERSPECTIVE ON CLARITY

The Start-Up
I wear ten different hats and am fighting to survive!

You are just getting started and in a small business, most people wear many hats—which is a definite clarity challenge. You are choosing to begin your business because you can see the bigger, brighter future! Make sure that you do not quickly become too busy to improve, as this can be a danger zone in a small business. What task can you accomplish or set in motion today that will make tomorrow more successful? Make tomorrow easier? If you have people working with you already, then ensure that you and your people know the one or two tasks that belong to them and how they lead to the one big goal of your business.

The Freelancer
I'm on my own, but I still need good results!

You're freelancing for a reason, so don't take projects just for the paycheck. Does the work build your skills, make you feel great, or allow you to meet great people? Or does it build your bank account for a goal or purpose above and beyond your rent? It can be easy to forget the things that you want to accomplish, so stop and reanalyze your freelance work to ensure it's getting you where you intended to go.

The CEO

I feel responsible for everything!

Make the bigger, multi-year plan and then chunk it down into stepping-stone goals and roles that must be filled. Relay the importance and impact of those stepping-stone goals and make the importance of the journey clear. Make sure that people stay connected to that big-picture goal and, most importantly, the milestones on the way to achieving it.

The New Manager

I was good at my job, but now how do I lead people?

Make sure that your team knows your talents and skills, and make sure you know theirs. Allow them to tell you how they can be of the most help to you. What are some of your personal goals, and how will you measure your success in reaching them? What are some of your team members' personal goals, and how is the project supporting them in attaining them? If your team has a great year, how will **you** know, and how will **they** know? What will you contribute to the team, and what will you expect from each member, in order to have that great year?

The Virtual Leader

Virtual should not equal remote.

Your people have more freedom than ever around how they approach their workday. Lean into that freedom and focus on attracting their best efforts. Things like clocking time or forcing specific working hours will repel talent. Make It Clear as a virtual manager by leaning into the freedom your virtual world creates. They have more choices; so make it clear why choosing to engage with you is a good choice. A virtual team engaged with the big goal and empowered to do immediate tasks will give their best effort—even without "looking over their shoulder."

The Middle Manager

How do I matter with so many people above me?

You must have clarity on the one big goal, and, equally important, you must have clarity on the role you and your team play in reaching the one big goal. You must manage and communicate ("sell") your role and its importance or impact to both your team and your management. Your piece matters. Your ability to communicate the value of your work develops future possibilities for yourself and your team members.

The Project Manager
I don't have anyone reporting to me!

Take the initiative. What will success look like for your project? How will success be measured? When it's not clear, build clarity and ask others to iterate on what you've proposed. If you don't know how your project fits into the bigger picture, ask questions. Options and opportunities—and more projects of the type you want—come only to those who rock their current projects, so make sure that's you!

Make It Clear vs. The Ping-Pong Pig

....

....

....

....

....

....

....

....

....

....

....

....

....

....

....

....

....

....

MAKE IT **FUN**

When I shared the outline for this book with a few friends and advisers, several asked, "Are you sure you want to talk about fun? Will people take you seriously? Is it reasonable to create the expectation that work is fun?" The more I discussed and hashed out ideas, the more I realized that fun is at the core of attraction... and that in Leadership by Attraction, *fun* has its own, very specific, definition. Fun must be *relevant, actual* fun.

> *"My boss told me to have a good day... so I went home."*
>
> —ANONYMOUS

One of my first jobs in banking was as a bank teller trainer at Colonial Bank in downtown Birmingham, Alabama. That summer, I was informed that a local athlete from Auburn, Bo Jackson would be working with me as a teller. I was new in town (and just learning about the Auburn–Alabama rivalry), but even I knew about Bo. As a college freshman, he was being talked about as the greatest athlete of all time. I couldn't fathom why someone who would soon be a professional football *and* baseball player would be excited to show up for my training, so I prepared to meet someone with a chip on their shoulder and a desire to be almost anywhere else. I couldn't blame him, I thought, and yet this did not sound like it would be fun for either of us.

On his first day, I was surprised to meet a smiling, energetic young man. He actually wanted to spend the day in training with me! That summer, all day, every day, Bo cashed checks, but he also built his fan base. He had a line from the moment the door opened to the moment the door locked. Day after day, Bo arrived determined to make it a good day—and maybe even to make being a bank teller a valuable step in his life journey. He may have been a basically quiet person, however each day he was friendly and gracious with customers and coworkers.

I have no idea if Bo remembers that time in his life, but I do, because I learned the importance of how you show up and the impact it has on everyone around you. That summer, everyone in that bank loved their job and every client loved their bank. Bo decided to Make It Fun when it certainly didn't have to be.

Fun begins with how you choose to show up: your smile, your energy, and how you face the day. But fun goes beyond this daily choice.

Make It Fun, like the other principles, takes intentionality and planning. You have to understand the value of fun and then pursue it. Fun does not have to be unprofessional or unproductive, and work doesn't have to suck!

So why is fun not associated more frequently with achieving goals, being productive, and working? All of these are good things, right? Do you feel guilty having fun because others aren't? Is it inappropriate to have fun at this time or place? Or are you out of energy or time for fun?

The right kind of fun breaks barriers, creates relationships, opens communication, and spurs interest. Your stressed-out, overbooked, uptight world is rampant with burnout, exhaustion, and an inability to focus. But the right kind of fun encourages productivity, job satisfaction, and profits!

FOCUSING FACTS

- 24% of an average person's lifespan will be spent at work, a total second only to sleeping.[14]
- Only 13% of worldwide employees are engaged at work.[15]
- 48% of Baby Boomers, 50% of Gen X, and 55% of Millennials report feeling disengaged at work.[16]

WHAT IS FUN?

"The opposite of play is not work, it is depression," says Brian Sutton-Smith, who researches the topic. Thank goodness you're not destined to spend so much of life not having fun.

Leadership by Attraction calls for a higher purpose for fun. It calls for *relevant* fun, and both of these aspects are critical. If your job aspires only to relevance, then it's just work. If it aspires only to fun, then it's trivial.

The Make It Fun principle is a call to make it relevant and fun. If what you do is fun *while* you are being productive, you and your team get to be effective and happy. When that happens, it's electric… and it's attractive.

---

14 Campbell, Lisa. "We've Broken Down Your Entire Life Into Years Spent Doing Tasks." Huffpost. Accessed: August 2020. https://www.huffingtonpost.com.au/2017/10/18/weve-broken-down-your-entire-life-into-years-spent-doing-tasks_a_23248153/

15 Rigoni, Brandon, and Nelson, Bailey. "Do Employees Really Know What's Expected of Them?" Gallup. Accessed: August 2020. https://news.gallup.com/businessjournal/195803/employees-really-know-expected.aspx

16 "How Millennials Want to Work and Live." Gallup. Accessed: August 2020. https://news.gallup.com/reports/189830/e.aspx

(+) ATTRACT

Relevant

Fun

Not Relevant

Not Fun

Relevant, and Fun
Optimal!

- Dream boards
- Field trips (experiential learning)
- Contests or awards
- Trivia (Include industry and office questions)
- Online scavenger hunt (Find info on vendor or industry sites)
- Speed dating for new roles or products

Fun, Not Relevant
Attractive but not optimal if not tied to vision

- Early happy hour during work time
- Holiday parties
- Golf outings
- Ping-pong tables

Relevant, Not Fun
May be necessary at times

- Boss "Meet and Greet" with no topic
- Reviewing results, data
- Quota setting
- Cross training
- Meeting or call of 90+ minutes with no break

Not Relevant, Not Fun
Should be avoided

- MasterMind with no topic or leader
- Late happy hour during personal time
- Policies with no rationale (e.g., dress codes)
- Paperwork, red tape, manuals

(-) REPEL

The attraction of relevant fun is it's engaging, energizing, and uplifting quality, often referred to as the team (or company) "culture." There's a lot of talk about the importance of culture. Everyone seems to agree that it's important and know when it's bad, but no one seems to understand how to build it. Culture is implicit rather than explicit, emotional rather than rational, and in many ways, it's difficult to measure. That's what makes it so hard to work with (or to work on), but it's also what makes it so powerful.

Culture is not just a management buzzword, nor is it an initiative to be accomplished. Culture, energy, engagement, buzz—this is the stuff of fun and of leadership.

WANTED

THE PARTY-POOPER PIG

- Hangs around those who say,
  - ▷ "Happy Friday."
  - ▷ "As soon as this class is over, I'll go have fun."
  - ▷ "If we need to have fun, just plan a happy hour."
  - ▷ "I just can't go through one more boring day here."

- Crimes:
  - ▷ Draining energy with numbing routine
  - ▷ Trudging and slogging through the days
  - ▷ Planning irrelevant fun that takes away from personal time

---

Party-Pooper Pig is wanted for eating all the energy. It trudges slowly through days with nothing to look forward to. It's big, heavy, boring, routine. It shows up, but it's just as happy not to be there at all.

Party-Pooper Pig plans things because "it's time," "they've always done it," or "we have to," and the plans are always unrelated to work. Activities where bonding is supposed to occur take place during people's personal and family time. Party-Pooper Pig squeals and snorts that fun is separate from work, confident that fun should never interfere with work.

Regularly dreading the office, anxiously awaiting the weekend, or just toiling through the day means there's nothing to look forward to. Failing to plan awards, competitions, offsite education and other relevant-fun activities means missed opportunities. Being present to complete tasks is hardly leadership. Believing work must be only labor isn't leadership either. Attractive leadership creates energy and enthusiasm *around* and *in* the work, the goals, and the tasks.

The burden of boredom is real. Who wants to just show up and toil? Attractive leaders create energy, buzz, and a dynamic environment. It can be easy to blame the job, the company, the role for boredom and routine. However, you must first look at your own leadership and the environment you create. Honestly consider your own energy and attitudes, the recognition offered and received, and celebrations or competitions planned. Are you a positive force? Do you need to hire or delegate in this area?

Attractive leaders have fun. Tasks won't all be fun, and every day doesn't need to be a load of laughs. However, it is important and, frankly, necessary for great results, that there be *something* to look forward to: something energizing, something engaging. At its best, something atypical or nonroutine. The words *work* and *fun* are not antonyms!

Zig Ziglar famously said, "People often say that motivation doesn't last. Well, neither does bathing, that's why we recommend it daily."

Cries of "We've got nothing to look forward to" become a Party-Pooper Pig that gets in the way of leaders being their most attractive. You're not at your best when you're bored, uninspired, and burdened with routine, and no one wants to follow that leader. Party-Pooper Pig is squealing and snorting that you just need to get through the day because fun comes later. Party-Pooper Pig invites you to feel great, but *only* after hours. And letting Party-Pooper win keeps you from Making It Happen in the most significant ways.

When energy and buzz become toil and drudgery, be careful: Party-Pooper Pig might be sitting right on top of you, squashing the joy out of your days!

WHY FUN ATTRACTS

The value of Make It Fun is obvious: people are attracted to fun and repelled by the boring and stressful. Did you know that April 3rd is Don't Go To Work If It Isn't Fun Day? Seriously.[17] It's no wonder that when I connect fun with leadership, it frequently comes out sounding trite.

So, what makes relevant fun so attractive? Let's look at the science of fun.

Common Knowledge	Hard Evidence for Having Fun
Fun makes people happier.	Fun releases dopamine, which promotes feelings of pleasure and satisfaction.
Fun helps teams connect.	Having fun with others builds trust and flexes communication muscles.[18]
Fun is a helpful distraction.	Memory and concentration are improved by reducing stress—aka having fun.[19]
Customers like having fun.	Pike's Place Market sells fish with a twist. Music and energy turn a smelly, regular job into a popular tourist destination. People come from around the world to purchase fish from employees having relevant fun.

17 National Don't Go to Work Unless It's Fun Day. Accessed: August 2020. https://www.checkiday.com/61c1ee19855156630c6ab8143f65dd40/national-dont-go-to-work-unless-its-fun-day

18 Everett, April. (2011). Benefits and Challenges of Fun in the Workplace. Library Leadership & Management; Vol 25, No 1 (2011). 25.

19 Everett, April. (2011). Benefits and Challenges of Fun in the Workplace. Library Leadership & Management; Vol 25, No 1 (2011). 25.

Fun gets more out of work.	Relevant fun establishes flow, the state of "being completely involved in an activity.... and you're using your skills to the utmost."[20]

Scientists recognize the importance of fun; why is it so hard for leaders? It's because fun is misunderstood. Fun is most effective—and most attractive—if it is legitimately both fun *and* relevant.

Bring fun back, because *fun matters.* Refusal to accept that fact by so many leaders is a great illustration of how hard it can be to get it right. Think about interviewing, which can be a negative, almost painful experience. If applying for that next position or promotion was fun instead of trying, how might the end result change for the better? Would better candidates be attracted?

If your business or project is a snooze-fest, or your team is filled with tension, noise, and competing personalities, then you'd better get to work having the right kind of fun.

DELOITTE'S CHALLENGE

Gamification introduces elements of game design into nongame applications to increase enjoyment, engagement, and retention. You'll find gamification on mobile apps, online communities, onboarding processes, and defensive driving curriculums (I know that personally). It's amazing what people do for points, achievement badges, filling a progress bar, or virtual currency.

---

20 Csikszentmihalyi, M. (1990). Flow: The Psychology of Optimal Experience. New York: Harper and Row

The Deloitte Leadership Academy is a famous case study in applying gamification to leadership development.[21] Deloitte designed an effective leadership training curriculum for senior executives, but there was no structured way to encourage executives to start and complete the program on their own time, not during the workday. Deloitte hired a company called Badgeville to create an innovative platform with a series of gamified elements—badges, leaderboards, and status symbols—for participating in and completing courses. When participants could see one another's scores and earn points, time to certification for participants dropped by 50%—they were motivated to move through the program and did so much more quickly.

Experiential learning is a trend for obvious reasons, including increased engagement, shared experiences among team members, and yes, the fun it provides!

WHERE FUN ATTRACTS

Relevant fun is not about your after-work activities. An attractive organization has a culture that buzzes with energy and is infused at critical points with relevant fun. Fun *while* you are being productive should be a part of the day-to-day journey in the work environment itself, in interactions with leaders, in special events, and in simple conversation. Fun should be visible, but how do you find it, encourage it, create it, and inject it?

CELEBRATE THE JOURNEY

Winning is fun. It feels good and it attracts people and results.

21 Bradt, George. "How Salesforce And Deloitte Tackle Employee Engagement With Gamification." Forbes. July 2013. https://www.forbes.com/sites/george-bradt/2013/07/03/how-salesforce-and-deloitte-tackle-employee-engagement-with-gamification

The issue is that you're not always winning, and sometimes you're flat-out losing. Reframe for intentional attraction by thinking of each step (whether starting, proceeding, achieving, or failing) as part of a journey to winning. Each step needs the attractive buzz created by relevant fun. Without it, people can feel overwhelmed by what's ahead, wither along a long path, or wilt in the face of defeat.

EASY: "WE DID IT!"

The obvious place to start celebrating the journey is a big achievement. Hit that sales quota? Make that big deadline? Achieve buy-in for a new idea? Deliver quality results? Celebrate! Seize these opportunities to refuel after a job well done. The path to achievement is almost always filled with stress, and while short bursts of stress bring people together, prolonged periods of stress tear them apart.

You could fill libraries with everything that's been written on the importance of celebrating big victories. This bar is low. There's no excuse not to get out there and have fun when you do something big.

HARDER: "WE'RE DOING IT!"

I once ran a contest to reward Realtors with the most listings. I thought it was a fun way to gamify a core part of the job and celebrate those who got the best results. After I'd run a few of these contests, though, someone on my team spoke up during a meeting.

"Why do we even do these? The Smiths always win. I mean, it's not fun for anyone else. I don't even think it's fun for the Smiths! They barely have to try!"

It was true, I realized. The contest hadn't done a good enough job of celebrating the *journey*. Yes, the Smiths were outstanding, but across hundreds of Realtors there was a lot of other good stuff to celebrate. I relaunched the contest with rewards that drove specific results *and* made it fun for more people: Most Improved, Most Consistent, Fastest Sale, Largest Sale, Sale with the Most Land, and—my personal favorite—The Lemon.

In no time, The Lemon became an office favorite, not because it singled out a low performer, but because it became a project for the whole team to help that person sell a low-priced listing with specific resources and action. Having the lowest-priced listing was no longer a point of frustration or shame. And the rebooted competition fostered teamwork, created more fun, and attracted results. It was a great example of celebrating the path and its stepping stones toward the ultimate goal. Everyone celebrated more listings, and we created teamwork in what is generally considered a competitive field.

While fun builds energy, it also requires energy to create. Even the healthiest team culture can become exhausting. *Relevant* fun sets the pace of energy and replenishes it too.

Gamification can add fun to education. Points, rewards, and competitions are a great path to fun. Think about online scavenger hunts to find answers or book clubs that read about business or creativity. Get creative in providing learning opportunities. When you become aware that additional education or learning needs to happen, stop and think about how you might Make It Fun.

Rewards and recognition don't have to be expensive. Get creative not only on what you are rewarding and recognizing, but also in how you are rewarding and recognizing. Some of the best rewards I've seen are professional kudos and advancement: a shout-out at the department meeting, an invitation to guest star in the monthly company video blog or write a column in the newsletter, a LinkedIn recommendation from the CEO, a personal coaching session, and so on.

And don't forget that growing together, creating together, feeling free to brainstorm—that's fun too!

How can you create meaningful milestones that are worth celebrating? Chunk goals down into meaningful steps, and celebrate each one.

HARDEST: "WE DIDN'T DO IT!"

With all the time and energy you put into *trying*, it can be particularly disappointing to fail—like running out of steam before crossing the finish line. Read too much about the wonder of failure and the joys of getting back up to try again, and you can easily forget that failure feels terrible. It feels wasteful (in terms of lost time and energy) and deflating (in terms of lost potential).

Is this really the time to throw a party? No. But failure doesn't mean you can't find the fun. Follow the journey, hear from the team, and show your own vulnerability and disappointment. In this moment fun, caring, and culture pull the right people closer together and increase the chances you'll get the right results next time around.

Next time you're afraid to share ideas remember someone once said in a meeting: "Let's make a film with a tornado full of sharks."

You took a swing and missed. Don't widen the plate with exceptions or excuses. This is not the time to break your own rules and give yourself the prize gated after success. That's not fun: that's cheating. Instead, help reframe, rebalance, re-encourage, and rise up. Genuinely praise and celebrate the effort.

And make sure you walk the walk. Don't talk about "failing forward" and "celebrating experimentation" only to deliver bad reviews and no bonuses. Faked fun is a serious repellent.

If you're recovering from failure, consider a field trip to a place that's doing it better than you are, perhaps succeeding in providing a higher level of service or a truly innovative product. Is now the time for a competition that would also improve skills?

It's also okay to celebrate the simple fact that tomorrow is another day, and you've learned a few things not to do next time. That in itself is worth a little fun.

CONSIDER YOUR IMPACT

When you are inspired, everyone should know. My mom had a saying framed in her bedroom: "Do you want your children drinking from a stagnant pond or a flowing river?" Energy and dynamism may be what you want, but are you, as the leader, providing it?

How does it feel to work with you? Is it slow and methodical, steady-as-she-goes, or fast and furious? When are you on, and when are you not? Honestly consider your personal impact on fun. If you give it your all on conference calls behind closed doors but then show fatigue to the rest of the office, is that the leader you intended to be?

FOOTBALL AFTER FOOTBALL

Watch Tony Romo broadcasting NFL games, and tell me he isn't loving it. There's a spike in ratings when he calls a game, and in a few short years, he has become the highest-paid sportscaster on TV.[22] He quickly went from being a leader on the football field to a leader in broadcasting. It's hard not to smile watching him because whether or not you like football, he is clearly having a great time. So you have fun too.

That fun is an attractor. While he is technically great at explaining the game, a master of stats, and a wizard at predicting the next play, that air of fun makes all the difference.

FUN CHECK

My husband has learned that when I'm scared, all fun stops. For everyone, when fear or exhaustion takeover there can be no fun.

My children learned to water-ski behind my brother's motorboat. They failed to launch time after time, face-planted at twenty miles per hour, and swallowed plenty of water along the journey. But eventually they could crisscross the wake and ski so long that my brother implemented a system called a Fun Check.

"Are you having fun?" he'd shout. "Do you want to go some more?"

This gave an opportunity for a thumbs-up or thumbs-down—keep going or that's enough.

Give your time, your money, and your attention to relevant fun. Then, see how it's going. Don't assume the fun you create is actually

---

22 New Details About Tony Romo's CBS Extension Reveal Total Worth of $180 Million. Dallas Morning News. Accessed August 2020: https://www.dallasnews.com/sports/cowboys/2020/02/29/tony-romos-new-contract-with-cbs-makes-him-the-highest-paid-nfl-analyst-in-tv-history/

fun... or remains fun. Keep checking. Keep caring. Keep focusing on fun. Because at the end of the day, it's your job to attract the right people to produce the right results. That means it's your job to have the right kind of fun. At the back of the book you'll find a Fun Check to assess where you are on creating relevant fun.

SUPPORT AN OFFICE BUZZ

A manager's chief job used to be employee oversight, ensuring that everyone was doing work. Someone had to keep an eye on water-cooler conversations and cafeteria chats to keep people focused, right? Even today, things like website blockers emphasize that company time is company money, and both should be spent on work.

Approximately 86% of office conversations are work-related.[23] People collaborate, ask for help, and break down silos across expertise areas. Shutting down the office buzz is actively shutting down productivity. It also sucks out fun.

In a virtual world, you must make the time and space for office buzz to happen. Before a meeting, open the virtual space early and allow people to stay on late, to allow for the more casual conversations to occur.

An organization's history, its institutional knowledge, is stored in the brains and memories of individuals. Through the stories they exchange, whether comparing experiences in the hallway, sharing info around the coffee station or discussing creating a background for themselves for the next virtual meeting, people often learn more than they do reading a company manual or studying a report.

---

23   The Upside of "Office Buzz" (or, "Stop Working and Start Talking!"). American Management Association. https://www.amanet.org/training/articles/the-upside-of-office-buzz-or-stop-working-and-start-talking.aspx

To build buzz and keep conversational fun relevant,

- Design attractive spaces for informal gatherings
- Leave unscheduled mix-n-mingle time on a conference schedule - or leave the virtual meeting open an extra 30 minutes and invite people to mix-n-mingle once you sign out.
- Create the time and space, either virtually or in person, for niche groups to gather and share

What can you do to build up that energetic buzz? Be visible, be present, be excited about what's next, and be available—just as you hope everyone working with you will be too. Encourage people to occasionally stop working and start talking!

MAKE IT OBVIOUS

Consider "making fun relevant" a creativity challenge. You can make anything relevant:

- Boss meet and greet? Connect to a hot topic for the company or project
- Happy hour? Connect drinks to a class on data visualization and a "what's the story?" challenge
- Reward? Connect to accomplishments or progress (see "celebrate the journey" above)
- Class? Set up a quiz show with prizes

There are different degrees of relevance, but when you get creative and obvious about finding relevance, you'll find that fun is suddenly more attractive. You might not always nail it, and you may accidentally decrease the overall fun at times, but that's better than giving up completely. Eventually you'll find what works for your team or project.

Sometimes the key to relevance is making sure everyone knows it's relevant. My real estate office once hosted some enthusiastic builders who wanted to talk to my agents, while providing food, wine, and prizes. It would certainly be fun, but without making the relevance obvious, it could have been nothing but a free happy hour.

Instead, the office staff circulated a reminder that this was put on by builders. If we wanted to have this fun event again, we'd better talk to them about building. Someone created a list of ten construction-related topics, and another person dared the office to restrict all discussion to those topics. It may not sound like it (Realtors can be a weird bunch), but the restrictions enhanced the fun while also ensuring relevance. People elbowed each other when conversation strayed. The result? Everyone had a good time and learned something new, and the event happened again because the builders found it valuable too. There's no one "right" way to relevance, but sometimes it's as easy as reminding people, "This is relevant because..."!

ENVIRONMENT AND ATMOSPHERE

Do not overlook the power of environment in attracting people and results. The environment you create can attract results, talent, team, and cohesion. That does not mean that every workspace needs a ping-pong table or a beer keg. In fact, those things can have fleeting value.

So, how do environment and atmosphere attract? Is it fun to enter your physical space? What about your virtual space? Do these environments match the message you mean to send? A vibrant atmosphere fosters interaction and a dynamic feeling of ideas being shared, challenges being overcome, and solutions being hatched!

Don't discount first impressions. Is there a contest going on? Did you just have a great month? Is there an upcoming holiday? How are phones answered and guests greeted? What's the wow factor when employees, clients, or guests enter your space? "May I get you a water or coffee?" doesn't pack much punch. But after your best month ever, give everyone you do business with a card with your amazing stats and a bite-sized PayDay candy bar. Guests share the success, clients want to be in business with the best, and employees have something to brag about!

Heat wave? Decorate your space with blue snowflakes, play "Frosty the Snowman," and put out a cooler full of Popsicles. Hang a sign reading, "We solve your problems, no matter the conditions!" Clients, vendors, and employees will notice, get energized, and even talk about it on social media.

KNOW WHERE YOU ARE

With both variables identified—fun and relevance—it's easy to see their presence or absence. Think back to the four quadrants of the fun and relevance chart discussed earlier.

REPELLING: NOT RELEVANT *AND* NOT FUN

Things that are not fun and not relevant are your enemy. They make people sigh, roll their eyes, look at their watches, and zone out completely. These repellents are culture detractors fueling the gossip, complaints, and toxicity that push good people and good results further away.

The complete absence of fun is desolate, woeful disengagement. It's everyone gone by five o'clock sharp and thin attendance at optional activities. It's emotional, but it's also trackable. Work may be getting done, but turnover is high, absenteeism is an issue, and work culture is toxic. People can't wait to get away. When attempts at fun are made, the sound of crickets rather than conversation can be embarrassing and frustrating.

One study that caught my attention was work by the founder and president of the National Institute for Play, Stuart Brown, who cataloged the backgrounds of more than six thousand people. He found that depriving children of fun leads to the development of psychopathologies[24]—that is, it could create murderers. Now, I'm not implying that a dull workplace creates serial killers, but you can avoid an atmosphere that creates a desire to slash and thwart your efforts!

POSERS: FUN, NOT RELEVANT *OR* RELEVANT, NOT FUN

Posers are activities, usually well-intentioned, that don't quite generate energy or create fun. They lack one of the two required elements for attraction and instead leave people unfulfilled, wondering why they wasted their time.

Activities with no relevance pose as fun. Happy hour is usually more fun with friends than with coworkers. Staff or team lunches can be a drag, and uninspired holiday parties put no one in the spirit. Even a ping-pong break can be a pain if it means you stay longer at the office for no real reason.[25] Perks like free food and games will only carry you so far. Activities without relevance can be attractive and help people find shared interests, but they aren't optimal.

Relevant activities with no fun pose as productivity. These activities may be necessary at times, but they aren't what attracts talent. Don't delude yourself: a meet and greet with the boss may be necessary, but

24 Bekoff, Mark. "The Importance of Play: Having Fun Must be Taken Seriously." Psychology Today. May 2014. https://www.psychologytoday.com/us/blog/animal-emotions/201405/the-importance-play-having-fun-must-be-taken-seriously

25 Elias, Jennifer. "New Study Shows What Bay Area Employees Want Most At Work (Hint: It's Not Ping Pong)" Silicon Valley Business Journal. June 2018. https://www.bizjournals.com/sanjose/news/2018/06/26/linkedin-workplace-study-want-employees-want.html

honestly, it's seldom fun. You're under pressure to show up and get some face time or, worse, afraid of being noted as absent. People want the boss to know who they are, and, oh gee, if they make a funny joke that gets 'em laughing, it's a total success.

It makes me think of one of my favorite managers, Michael Scott from *The Office*. He's a great example of someone who just can't nail the fun. With Michael, there's no in-between: he's either planning eye-roll inducing attempts at fun that distract from productivity or undermining what little fun can be found in office drudgery. Both choices repel, and yet mercifully his perseverance eventually lands a few wins. He cares about the office culture, and so he cares about attraction.

ATTRACTIVE: RELEVANT AND FUN

Once you have it, don't take it for granted. This is not simply culture; it's important work for you and the wider team. Fun is at its finest when there's *easy* intentionality. Time spent cultivating fun is time spent attracting the right people and thus the right results.

People are attracted to relevant fun. If they're going to spend all this time with colleagues, how can you tap into a desire for self-improvement or positive social impact? Creating an energetic culture of growth and excellence will make things fun.

START ATTRACTING

Look ahead to *Passing Your Pigs* in Part 2 for a self-assessment of where you are with Making It Fun.

Fun is not an escape. You're not working for the weekend, or happy hour, or the five o'clock bell. That mentality does not attract good people or yield good results. While work time may never have the importance or the joy of family and friend time, it also doesn't need to be a prison of gloom and doom.

At best, the working-for-the-weekend mentality leads to a neutral work culture where Friday interactions always begin with a "Happy Friday to you." At worst, it's deep-seated hatred of time spent at work, where getting off the clock really is a meaningful unshackling.

Because those aren't attractive qualities, making fun relevant and making relevant fun are all about intentional action, which begins with an awareness of what work needs to be done. The exercises in Part 2 help assess your fun factor and start attracting with intentional action.

New project? New role? New company? Feeling stagnant? Feeling overwhelmed? Try it out to see how much fun exists and how it might help attract people and results.

Fun is a basic human need, but all too often it falls outside a leader's purview, either because it's "not worth their time" or "needs to happen organically." Leaders may even forget to show up each day, ready for fun. That's baloney. Leaders who attract people and get results focus on relevant fun. Give your money, your time, and your encouragement to fun, and you'll notice the improvement. Bo Jackson didn't gain his fame and fortune being a bank teller, but his embrace of relevant fun came shining through every day. Does yours?

FIND YOUR PERSPECTIVE ON FUN

The Start-Up
I wear ten different hats and am fighting to survive!

Because you're a start-up, you may face budget challenges in planning fun. Don't forget the power and the warm feeling of simply saying thank you. Slow down and de-stress with the people who may be a part of your eventual success. That may mean employees, but in the start-up world, it can also be a vendor that goes above and beyond or someone in a related industry who has taken an interest in your business. Say thank you, and find time to unwind together, even if it's in a small way, for a few moments. Don't overlook fun because you're too focused on survival. People will feel the goodwill, send referrals and think of you positively!"

The Freelancer
I'm on my own, but I still need good results!

Find associations or groups that provide relevant, fun activities. Freedom may have been your goal, but isolation is tough; seek out others who share the same industry or the freelance lifestyle. When you are hired to consult and contribute, are they glad they chose you? Do you show up with energy and a smile, adding to the fun?

The CEO
I feel responsible for everything!

Is my company perceived as the fun, happening place that people are tripping over each other to join or the tired company that people can't wait to leave? Answer this question honestly. Planning big fun that is truly fun for most participants can be very challenging. Start small and do some fun checks. Does each department have at least some budget for relevant fun? Is each team committed to relevant fun—and is it a part of your accountability check-ins? Set an expectation that fun will be had which will help assure that your team enjoys some relevant fun together.

The New Manager
I was good at my job, but now how do I lead people?

Get creative. This is a great way to Make It Yours. Begin by adding in a few things that you find fun and relevant, and then get to know your new team by letting them take the lead in turn and Make It Theirs. In your excitement about your new role, don't forget that energy and buzz around fun that is relevant is a best first step. Are they showing energy and anticipation each time you are leading? Bring it!

The Virtual Leader
Virtual should not equal remote.

Remember that your energy and passion show through an online meeting too - so be sure that you bring it, which will make it easier to expect them to bring it too! You can create energy in some simple ways like music as you enter, or a virtual background competition, or a quote of the day - just as you would for an in-person gathering. You'll know if you face screens with the camera off and their microphone muted that you are not getting engagement. They do not expect the meeting to be fun, energetic or important. They have already decided not to bring their best efforts to your online gathering. Reflect on that and decide how to best attract their engagement through a guest presenter, some competition or better questions that encourage active dialogue between participants. Don't forget to emphasize the increased fun that is occurring due to work at home - at the end of the meeting or the end of the day, they are already with their family or ready for personal time!

The Middle Manager
How do I matter with so many people above me?

Remind your team that they *are* a team by planning relevant fun. Set up a thank-you celebration just for them. Create pride in their group and their achievements. Don't let them get lost in a bigger organization. Consider inviting your boss to the fun, too. And prepare for other talented people to want to join your fun team!

The Project Manager

I don't have anyone reporting to me!

In this role, you may not be able to wait for relevant fun to come to you. Go find it, or help create it. Are there related teams or departments that you could get to know better? Can you be the leader of all or part of a relevant fun event? Whether your project is long term or short term, you'll have more options in your next assignment if you bring some fun into this one.

Make It Fun vs. The Party-Pooper Pig

MAKE IT **YOURS**

I was born and raised in High Point, North Carolina, and went to college only thirty minutes away. When I got married, we moved to Nashville, Los Angeles, and then Birmingham, but moving to New Orleans—despite being back in the South and closer to my original home—felt like moving to a foreign country. It wasn't just another move. New Orleans had unique accents, different customs, new things to eat (crawfish?! boudin?!), and yes, new things to drink everywhere. Amid all this change, one thing was clear: this was my new home.

> *"My mission in life is not merely to survive, but to thrive; and to do so with some passion, some compassion, some humor, and some style."*
>
> —MAYA ANGELOU

My first objective? Find a job. A newspaper ad showed a bank teller opening at a local bank. I didn't really want to be a bank teller, but after my experience working with Bo, there was a job at a bank that I did want. I just needed to make it mine. So, I planned how I might guide the interview to discuss my ideal banking job.

I walked into the interview determined to ask for what I wanted. Then things became intimidating. My appointment was in the main branch office. This bank had several satellite offices, and it was clear that things were well put together, organized, and classy. How could I walk into this established environment, talk to the bank president, and expect to do whatever I wanted?

My name was called. I entered the bank president's office. He was a friendly Louisiana native, and at nine in the morning, he offered me a drink (and he didn't mean a coffee). I loosened up and also became more determined. This would certainly be different than my past experiences, and it was certainly someplace I'd like to work.

Conversation about weather and traffic quickly passed, and then came the first real interview question: "Why do you want to be a bank teller here?"

Obvious and simple, and yet I knew I needed to answer my way.

"I love helping people understand finances, but the industry also interests me. There's so much new technology in the space. Customers are embracing the ease and efficiency of automation, and that's going to keep changing things. I would certainly enjoy being a good bank teller for you, but what I'd really love to do is be a bit more than that—a real ambassador for your bank. Someone to promote automation while working with the staff and officers to maintain the relationships too. Would there be a way for me to do that for you?"

The bank president leaned back, took a swig of not-coffee, and then replied, "I guess you might need to tell me more about that."

And so I walked out of an interview for a position as a bank teller with a newly created role as the business development officer. I had the chance to make this role my own, and I had taken one big step to making this bank and New Orleans my new home.

This was a unique moment, but doesn't every opportunity and every role—indeed, every day—contain the chance to Make It Yours? Sure, there are tasks to be done and goals to be met, but then what?

During my time as the business development officer in LaPlace,

Louisiana, I learned a critical concept for my future: lagniappe. I received it (like getting thirteen donuts when I only paid for twelve), and the bank president pushed me to figure out how it could be given, and shown, to our clients. What "little something extra" or "little something special" could be done today?

What—in your experience, your skills, your hobbies, your strengths—can make how *you* do your work different than how anyone else might do it?

That's how you Make It Yours: a little something extra; a little bit different. Adding lagniappe to your leadership will attract others who want to add something of theirs too.

FOCUSING FACTS

- About two-thirds of managers are either not engaged or actively disengaged in their work.[26]

- The word *authentic* comes from the Greek word for "author."

- Authenticity leads to happiness and psychological well-being.[27]

- 25% of workers in the United States will be 55 or older by 2024. In 1994 only 10% of workers were 55 or older.[28]

- Only 18% of employees feel they work in "transparent" workplaces.[29]

---

26 Harter, James. "If Your Managers Aren't Engaged, Your Employees Won't Be Either." Harvard Business Review. Accessed August 2020: https://hbr.org/2019/06/if-your-managers-arent-engaged-your-employees-wont-be-either

27 Brafman, Rom. "Does Authenticity Lead to Happiness? Authenticity and Happiness: A Real Link." Psychology Today. Accessed August 2020: https://www.psychologytoday.com/us/blog/dont-be-swayed/200808/does-authenticity-lead-happiness

28 Volini, Erica. "Learning in the flow of life: 2019 Global Human Capital Trends." Deloitte. Accessed August 2020: https://www2.deloitte.com/us/en/insights/focus/human-capital-trends/2019/reskilling-upskilling-the-future-of-learning-and-development.html

29 Volini, Erica. "Leadership for the 21st century: The intersection of the traditional and the new." Accessed: August 2020: https://www2.deloitte.com/us/en/insights/focus/human-capital-trends/2019/21st-century-leadership-challenges-and-development.html

WHAT IS MAKING IT YOURS?

When I think about the specifics of Making It Yours, I focus on two words and really break them down: *extraordinary* and *remarkable*. This sounds daunting because sometimes these words imply "amazing," "miraculous," or "astounding." That's attractive but hardly required for Leadership by Attraction.

Instead, I punctuate to "extra-ordinary" and "remark-able." Add something extra to the ordinary or elicit comments about whatever you're doing. You don't have to bedazzle, just earn a remark: "My bank surprised me," "This is cool about where I work," "I didn't expect that in my project's goals," or "I thought today would be a dull meeting, but it went by really fast."

Remember, Leadership by Attraction is not a recipe to become a certain type of leader. It's not about pleasing or influencing everyone. These lenses help leaders of all types attract the right people and results. So Make It Yours by adding your little something extra.

BEFORE GOOGLE: THE ARTOM COLLECTION

While I attended Wake Forest University, I worked in the library's Artom Collection. It was not a highly sought-after job because it was in a dark basement, sitting among rows and rows of file cabinets, reading magazines and newspapers. When I first started, there were days when I did not see or hear another person during my shift. But I loved it. With each day that passed, I loved even more that I could make the job my own. My role was to read the periodicals, cut out and copy articles, and file them by subject matter. Yep, I was Google before Google existed. The idea was that students studying a topic could come to the collection and easily find recent articles about that subject.

I quickly realized that the job had not been done the way I really wanted to do it, and that the students didn't even know the collection existed. In my opinion, this valuable resource was basically being wasted. So I started highlighting the topics or subjects where an article could be filed. Sometimes I made five or six copies of the same article and filed it under multiple subjects. The files got thicker, and the ways to think about topics got broader. Because I am social by nature, I started telling everyone about it —and they told others—and sure enough, usage went up. I worked in the Artom Collection for two and a half years, and after the first few months, I was rarely alone any more. And I am convinced that I had some of the most interesting conversations on campus!

To take it one step further, reading about current events for my "boring" basement job led me to apply for an independent study my senior year as a step toward receiving my degree in Economics. I was fortunate to spend a semester researching the topic of national health insurance with Dr. John C. Moorhouse, investigating its positives, negatives, and likely impact. That was in the eighties, and since some things change and some things stay the same: that research remains an interesting reference in conversations today.

WANTED

THE PARKED PIG

- Hangs around those who say,
  - ▷ "I don't care anymore."
  - ▷ "I just want my paycheck."
  - ▷ "I'm counting down to the day I can leave."

- Crimes:
  - ▷ Stagnation
  - ▷ Apathetic contentment
  - ▷ Just occupying a position or title, not mattering to the role
  - ▷ Too much daydreaming without doing

Parked Pig is wanted for loitering. It's unmotivated, unwilling, or unable to get a move on. Parked Pig wants to do as little as possible to get by and may even think everyone feels that way. Work is work, right? Parked Pig actually poisons contentment, turning it into settling. Sure, the basics may get done, but it's more interested in marking time than making progress.

Parked Pig is average, and attractive leaders are *not* average!

A job (or role) is different from a career, different from a business, different from a passion, and different from a purpose. Thinking about why you do what you do, or why others might want to work with you, can feel overwhelming and unproductive. Parked Pig can make it seem easier to focus on the activities of the job rather than creating something with passion and purpose. Parked Pig wants you to leave your own talents, skills, and passions at home. Parked Pig prevents you from finding satisfaction and fulfillment in a role or situation by telling you that just doing the tasks is enough.

You cannot be a distant leader, even in the instances where you are leading using virtual tools. Distance expands when you realize you're only showing up for a paycheck. Maybe you have no interest or no part to play in the big goal. Maybe you have no energy left for learning more or staying current. Maybe you have lost your belief that you matter to the big picture or to those around you. Leaders with these feelings are unattractive.

Apathy becomes the Parked Pig, leaving us bored, frustrated, underutilized, and unchallenged. Going through the motions—especially when you're a capable leader—can fail to engage your caring, talents, and passion.

When the leader isn't contributing talent and energy, why would anyone else?

When passion and purpose become distant, you've got a Parked Pig. It's squealing and snorting that this role, or this project, or this company isn't worth your effort. And Parked Pig thinks no one will notice that you're not bringing your best. It rolls in average mud—whatever mud happens to be there—and wants you to do the same.

WHY MAKING IT YOURS ATTRACTS

Leaders of all types attract, so you be you! While participating in the development of the Keller Personality Assessment used to assess the most natural fit for certain roles within Keller Williams Realty, I studied a variety of personality profile tests. Intelligent and ambitious people can succeed in many ways that may not be a natural fit, but it is easiest when you can be you. Using the Myers-Briggs personality assessment, Steve Jobs was considered an INTJ—introverted, driven. He led with a brilliant mind for design rather than an openly charming wit. Oprah Winfrey is considered an ENFJ—extroverted and honest. She leads through people and optimism. Some leaders will be primarily analytical and methodical. Others will be fast-moving and confident. Quincy Jones once said: "Imagine what a harmonious world it could be if every single person, both young and old, shared a little of what he is good at."

Things change so quickly that leaders must lead amid volatility. Inauthentic leaders struggle to keep up due to the effort that goes into faking their responses. Authentic leadership lets you adapt more effortlessly.

Learn who you really are. How do you prefer to think, act, socialize, process information, and so on? Acknowledge and act upon these strengths and weaknesses. Then, make time to learn about those most important to your success. By understanding yourself and others, you are preparing to take action when needed.

Gallup's Strengths Coaching certification program reports that

- People who focus on their strengths are three times more likely to report having an excellent quality of life.

- Those who use their strengths every day are six times more likely to be engaged at work.

- Teams that focus on strengths are 12.5% more productive.

A recent Harris Poll commissioned by Healthy Companies International found that a strong majority of Americans believe that conscious leaders—those who are aware of themselves, others, and their surroundings—can vastly improve organizational productivity and profitability. Research suggests that many feel the world is changing faster than their organization can adapt and that more conscious leaders are needed to guide teams through this acceleration.[30]

Have you heard, "If you love what you do, you never have to work a day in your life?" or "Do what you love and the money will follow?" Turning a passion into a career isn't always possible, but it's realistic to inject that passion into your career.

If you love to write, be the one to draft copy for a big project. If you rock out with your band on the weekends, provide music for marketing videos or the dreaded holiday party. Love photography? Document the year, the project, new hires, or whatever else might add value. So if you love to act or are a great public speaker, then speak – and make videos too. Will your marathon training inspire others? Do you have a green thumb so that you could adopt-a-space?

Lagniappe (Lan • Yap): A little Something Special

Incorporating your passions could help you feel less stressed, more personally fulfilled, or more valuable. It may increase your creativity and your problem solving on the job. It certainly makes you more interesting. And it just may help you build connections with others. So, bring the real you into your work, and enjoy the results!

---

30 New Healthy Companies/Harris Poll: Employees Want More 'Conscious' Leaders. Accessed: August 2020. https://healthycompanies.com/wp-content/uploads/2018/07/HCI-Harris-Poll-Release-FINAL-07-16-2018.pdf

What is your lagniappe? Where can you bring that to your leadership? Where do you need to Make It Yours and succeed using your unique qualities, strengths, passions, and interests?

WHERE MAKING IT YOURS ATTRACTS

Being miraculous sounds hard, but being extra-ordinary and re-mark-able are easy. Bring your little something extra to attract a whole lot extra. Make It Yours and be authentic, keep growing, and think big.

BE AUTHENTIC

Authenticity has been written about frequently, and research shows that authenticity boosts productivity and creates a positive work environment.[31] Leadership by Attraction keeps authenticity simple: you *need* to be you. Intentionally be yourself in your strengths and your vulnerabilities.

AUTHENTIC STRENGTH

Albert Einstein once said, "Everybody is a genius, but if you define a fish by its ability to climb a tree, it will live its whole life believing it is stupid." Are you clear on your strengths? Your talents? What you're best at? Can you identify things you love and why?

Lean into your strengths. Leadership by Attraction brings focus to areas where you are the best, or the most, or the biggest, or at least that you enjoy. The pursuit of excellence is interesting, relatable… and an attractor. So when you as a leader are pursuing excellence, *expecting* excellence, that is an attractor, right up until it's pressure.

---

31   "Most Employees Feel Authentic at Work, but It Can Take a While." Harvard Business Review, 2016. Accessed August 2020: https://hbr.org/2016/05/most-employees-feel-authentic-at-work-but-it-can-take-a-while

It's not enough just to demand excellence; that isn't really Making It Yours.

Get serious about including people in a way that interests you. It's not about being a cheerleader or making a show out of being interested. Remember we're talking about being authentic. Do an intentional and serious check: why are days different (better) when you are there?

I like to imagine a herd of zebras. I can identify them from afar as zebras, their physiques are similar and they are all recognizable as zebras! And yet, no two zebras have the same stripes. Each animal's stripes are as unique as our own human fingerprints. When you are using an authentic strength, it is not just what you are good at, but also about what fulfills you, and what brings out the passion in you. Two people may receive the same training and show up with the same proficiency – but it may be an area of authentic strength for one and not for the other.

Some strengths may not seem relevant, but Making It Yours is about showing who you are. It is okay to earn a reputation as an outside-the-box thinker. In our world that can be too full of comparisons, it is attractive to be comfortable and confident in being yourself. Demonstrating your interests and your strengths, sharing your gifts with the world, is not just a trite phrase, it is a secret that helps you create an environment where others feel encouraged to share their gifts, their talents and their strengths too.

Nelson Mandela reminded us of the leadership power of being authentic, and letting our strengths shine: "As we let our own light shine, we unconsciously give other people permission to do the same." Be open, listen and stay flexible so that you will notice those around you who may be raising their hand looking for ways to share their strengths, too. There's something extra-ordinary and remark-able about a leader who lets their light shine, and then allows others to shine too.

AUTHENTIC VULNERABILITY

It's impossible to achieve excellence without vulnerability. Being self-aware enough to know when to ask for help attracts people who can contribute to your success. Vulnerability is not weakness. It's strength in recognizing your weakness and attracting help. In this way, authentic vulnerability is very much a part of authentic strength, not something separate.

Spot opportunities for attractive vulnerability by looking for signs that you are being inauthentic: you feel awkward, you're fudging, taking shortcuts, undermining a coworker, not admitting mistakes, checking Facebook during meetings, disengaged with highs and lows of work, or pleasing others only so they will go away.

Suddenly, it's clear why vulnerability isn't weakness; it's courage, and it takes practice. Learning how and when to give feedback so the relationship grows is a learned skill. Learning how and when to relax and discuss something a bit personal is a learned skill. Finding ways and opportunities to be yourself, and to share yourself, takes practice.

Isn't it interesting that when you decide to be yourself, you leave your comfort zone behind? It is not always easy or natural to open up and share your passions with a group. There's no guarantee they'll be appreciative or receptive. It's tough when no one laughs at your jokes, but it's worth it. You are attracting talent to your journey and attracting big results. When you are open and vulnerable, you create an atmosphere that respects sharing, invites failure, and encourages openness and innovation. You demonstrate and create trust.

Remember, you aren't trying to attract everyone. You're attracting *your* people: those who want to share *your* journey, to be part of *your* story.

At the beginning of her career, Oprah Winfrey found it difficult to detach from the news stories she was reporting. She was seen as too emotional, not newsy enough, so she was moved off prime-time news and into daytime TV—a big demotion. And the rest is history.

KEEP GROWING

Most leaders get to their role for a specific reason. Maybe an advanced skill, proven dependability, or expertise led to past success. For whatever reason, now they're leading others, sometimes people who used to be peers.

When I ran for a position on the Lewisville, Texas, school board, I wanted my two children to get the best possible education. Of course, I believed my ideas and values would benefit all children, but my focus was on a few limited issues, like how elementary school grades were given and how a high-school GPA would be calculated.

"I had no idea that being your authentic self could make me as rich as I've become."

— OPRAH WINFREY

My beliefs were shared by enough people to get me elected. Soon after the election, one of the administrators who had not supported me asked if we could go to lunch.

This will be sweet, I thought. We went to lunch and had an open conversation. I'm sure he felt passion when I shared my specific issues, and he listened with kindness and curiosity.

At the end of lunch, he told me he liked me and looked forward to working with me. And then he shared something I didn't understand fully at the time, something I'll never forget because it's proved true in almost all leadership situations: "Most people have a reason they run for office, and if we get really lucky, they outgrow it."

I went on to work on my issues. I kept promises, stayed true to my values, and also realized there was *a lot* I did not know about operating a public school district. To do this leadership role justice, I needed to study, learn, and grow. Eventually I became school board president, and I was challenged by an unprecedented change in my reason for office.

Almost two years after my election, on April 20, 1999, the tragic Columbine High School shooting occurred. Immediately, my issues felt small. They *were* small. The only priority became school safety, and it was a scary, shocking wake-up call. Overnight, all my past knowledge, experience, and expertise proved painfully unable to create a solution.

Leading now meant attending FBI-led trainings about school safety drills, collaborating with cities and towns for school resource officers, and talking with scared parents. As a leader and influencer, my growth became imperative. The day after the shooting—a Wednesday—schools were near empty. No one felt safe sending their kids to school due to uncertainty about what was happening and fears of copycats.

It was understandable. I shared those same feelings, and yet kids needed to go to school. It was hardly a time for school finance details, but the school district needed students. The sudden spike in school safety costs required a budget increase, and funding came in per-pupil allotments. If parents kept kids at home, their fears would be more likely to be realized because the district wouldn't be able to afford safety precautions.

The most important thing was to make school campuses as safe as humanly possible. Next, we needed to publicize what was being done to give families the confidence to send their children back to school. Every day brought decisions about new policies, new tools, and when/if/how to allow students to assemble for events such as graduation ceremonies.

This challenge remains pressing today, but in that moment, our school district needed to make it ours by growing, learning, and changing to meet a new reality. Equally, we needed to share openly that we *were* growing, learning, and changing. Returning to the same systems and processes wasn't an acceptable plan.

Leadership demands a willingness to admit that you don't know enough, that you don't have all the answers, and that you aren't prepared with quick and easy solutions. While virtual classrooms may solve school shooting challenges, they present a new reality and new challenges and new pressing needs for leaders to keep growing. Make It Yours by showing an unwavering commitment to personal growth and learning.

That commitment creates attraction. Learning means that you aren't stuck on yesterday's issues or solutions. It illustrates how you will find a path forward. Outgrowing your reason, along with the talent and skill that got you there, attracts as you move forward into whatever may come.

When you step into leadership, you cannot anticipate the challenges that will need your attention, the personalities that will make up your days, or the skills required for success. When's the last time you learned something new? Planning for and pursuing continual growth is both extra-ordinary and remark-able: it is Leadership by Attraction.

THINK BIG

Most people never get what they want because they never decide what they want. Make It Yours by setting an intentionally big vision for yourself and for your project, team, or organization—or all three. If a big vision has been set by the organization already, where does your team fit? How does your personal vision fit into the bigger vision? Who and what about the vision attracted you to this role, job, or project? Be prepared to share and to inspire. A big vision cannot be achieved without attracting the right help!

The best talent aspires to have an impact. People want room for their contributions. They want to spend days shooting for the moon, which guarantees that they'll land among the stars.

Visionary leaders attract people who aim high and work hard to reach the destination. A small vision doesn't require—or even access—the capabilities of those around you because it demands little in terms of ambition and resources. A big vision inspires excitement at the prospect of success and loyalty when times get tough. It sets high expectations for the leader and the team. Don't settle! You will recognize people who genuinely expect the best for you and from you—and those relationships are golden.

CREATING A BIG VISION

To attract people and results, Make It Yours by thinking big. Stake a claim to what you will achieve, knowing a big vision attracts the best talent.

Something truly big:

- **Looks impossible from the outside.** It's not immediately obvious how something big will be accomplished; if you can see each step of the path to success, you aren't thinking big enough. Leave a space for the talents you want to attract to give their all in pursuit of the goal.

- **Connects the why, not the how.** Think of your big vision not as turn-by-turn directions, but rather as the *X* on the map. This creates opportunities for innovation and allows the different talents on your team to zigzag their way to the end.

- **Has staying power.** Accommodate changes without breaking. Don't focus too closely on one competitor, one cultural fad, one achievable number, or one anything that will come and inevitably go.

- **Creates a picture that can be seen, felt, measured, and imagined in full.** If you're wildly successful, how will you know? How will the world be different? How will you be different? If people can't envision the end, it is not easy to stay the course.

AVERSION TO BIG VISIONS

I've met too many people whose vision for themselves is small, sometimes much smaller than what I can see for them.

They'll say things like "I don't want to seem ungrateful." But who defined ambition as ungratefulness? When did you begin to believe that wanting more meant you did not, or could not, be grateful and appreciative of what you have today?

It's not unusual to feel uncomfortable setting goals only of things you want to buy or places you want to go. It can feel selfish to have a vision of some award you want to win. Creating a big vision can and should be more than a list of things you want—although things you want can be great stepping-stone goals on the way to the bigger vision. Creating that bigger vision should be about imagining and envisioning the story people will tell about you, in this leadership role and beyond. Creating a big vision should include the others who will be affected by your vision. Your vision can be a mesh of personal and professional, and in fact, for most people it is.

Deciding what you want, and being comfortable talking about it, can be challenging. You may be limited by your belief that you already have more than you dreamed or more than others in your family. Some around you may genuinely believe that something bigger is impossible or wrong for you. Be it jealousy, miseducation, or inexperience, when you're surrounded by people with small visions, it rubs off on you. You may also have a strong fear of failure, perhaps due to past experience, and that can be a powerful driver toward a smaller and safer vision.

Think further out, imagine bigger, and then work backward to a smaller, more immediate first step. I like to create a vision, or accomplishments, that are further out in time—and then chunk that down to what a next step can be.

Creating a big vision may be done individually (for example, if you're the only current employee) or with your immediate team. Either way, before locking it in, ask people what they think. Look for attraction as you share. Something big inspires conversation: "How the hell will you accomplish that?" It encourages ideas: "I know somebody you should talk to." And it draws out energy: "Oh, you could [xyz]!"

Solidifying your vision allows you to communicate it with enthusiasm and confidence, which is necessary in attracting others to your vision.

REPELLENT: TOO PERSONAL

Work friendships are an important—and often enjoyable—part of leadership. But how do you know if, or when, it's too much? Good leadership attracts hands, and heads, and hearts. You want to bring your whole self to work, right? You want that for others too, right?

Yes, but it's still work, so you'll want to leave *Fifty Shades of Grey* at home. How do you know where the boundaries lie? Here are a few questions for your consideration.

- Does what you are sharing make people seriously question your capabilities? Remember that you want them to see you as their leader.

- Does what you are sharing make someone else look less capable? Gossip in the workplace is always inappropriate.

- Are you talking about sex? Don't. Just don't.

- Are your people asking for help or just venting? Are you? Life is messy. When people stop bringing you their troubles, you quit being their leader. But they should respect you and your role enough to make an appointment that can be kept in privacy and on schedule. Practice redirecting venting into action, and focus conversations on results. Be prepared to give time off if absolutely necessary.

- Are you creating connections or entertainment? Building rapport by treating coworkers as interesting people is not the same thing as oversharing. Be cautious in what you choose to share and what you choose to listen to. There will be times when just changing the subject or moving to a different conversation is your best leadership move.

KNOW WHERE YOU ARE

Who in your life would you bend over backwards to help? When those people call me, my answer is always, "If I can, I will." Who feels that way about you? Make It Yours is the principle that creates those long-lasting relationships. They're not always your best friends or even people you see often, but these people have mattered in your life and you have mattered in theirs.

You don't Make It Yours just by showing up. Making It Yours requires vigilance and intentional authenticity, growth, and big thinking. These qualities let *you* attract *your* right talent to achieve *your* right results. So, with intentionality moving you forward, start by understanding where you are today.

The following situations and charts highlight ways to Make It Yours. Every leader will experience all of these because the world, and the organization, and the project, and the people will change. The trick is to maximize your attraction by recognizing repellents and take action accordingly. As you read, think about where you are right now.

DISTANT: IT'S NOT YOURS

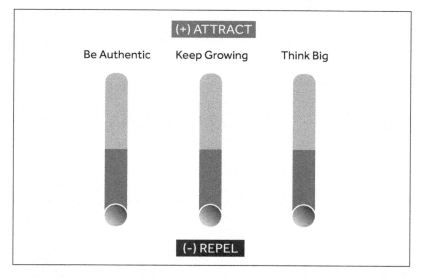

You are in the Distant phase when you fail to Make It Yours: you are not authentic, not growing, and/or not thinking big, for one or more of many possible reasons.

Maybe you aren't able to be yourself. Maybe you aren't growing. Maybe you're thinking too small and failing to attract big help. Maybe you didn't set the vision yourself. Maybe you feel restricted in sharing your strengths or vulnerabilities. Maybe you're just too tired.

Whatever the cause, you feel distant from your leadership role. You're simply going through the motions, and when that's the case, you aren't attracted to your own role, much less attracting others to support you! Even when you bring cupcakes, no one really cares. Big talent has diverted to some other, more attractive challenge, team, or leader, and those who are left are just going through the motions. This is a decision moment. Do you take steps to Make It Yours? Do you move on? Remaining distant and disconnected is not an option in Leadership by Attraction.

COMPLACENT: AUTHENTICITY

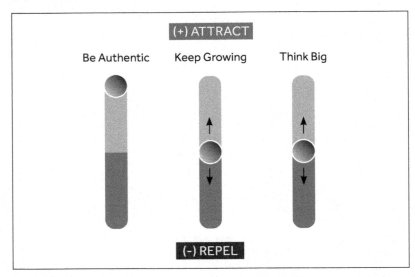

Familiarity breeds complacency. Your team knows you, supports you, loves you. Maybe they'd walk through fire for you. That doesn't necessarily mean you're growing or thinking big.

The Complacent phase is most often when you'll experience shock that people are bored, disgruntled, or not bringing their best each day. Team members may begin to make excuses for sloppy work and expect understanding for mistakes. Corners are cut, sick days are used liberally… people are just too comfortable with you. You may feel your own pace slowing as the need for urgency diminishes; you know you can get it done, so why push? But in this phase, other attractive forces may entice your team away. Something new, different, shiny, and *attractive* permits more growth or more opportunity. This situation is painful and difficult for everyone!

Monitor for complacency. If you feel complacent, comfortable, or lacking in challenge, you can bet that those around you do too. Fight off complacency by hosting brainstorming or MasterMind sessions that generate fresh ideas and new action. Talk about it openly: "We are awesome, and we want to stay awesome. So how do we do that? What can I do to help us stay awesome?" Find new education or a new presenter, and realize that it is a *fight* to avert repelling through complacency. When you suspect you and your team may be falling into complacency, that's the perfect time to revisit the five principles of Leadership by Attraction.

RENEWAL: GROWING

During this phase you are growing. Maybe you're improving skills around new necessary tasks, or maybe you're focused on learning about new people in your world. Either way, your growth is demonstrating your commitment to the role. Here, Authenticity and Big Thinking are in flux. It's not clear how authentic you are or can be, nor do you have time or ability to think big.

This phase can occur when you take on a new role, when the responsibilities that belong to you shift, or when a supporting team member changes. It can even occur when a key piece of technology or some aspect or process in your own role changes.

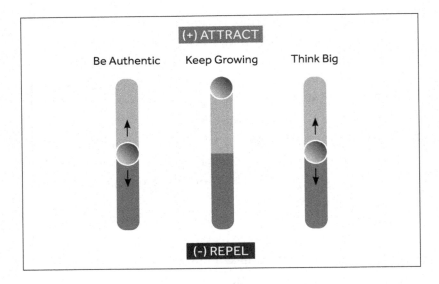

Since growth is a given, concentrate on how you be authentic and think big. Build trust by exposing weaknesses: others may feel the same. You can increase authenticity just by sharing plans for your learning. What courses will you take? What time will you spend with each individual? What team-building exercises will you lead?

In this phase, you should radiate confidence in your ability to learn, and to lead, without arrogance. If you're paying close attention, you may be surprised at how often you visit this phase!

FRESH START: THINKING BIG

A fresh start is accompanied by a wholehearted focus on big thinking. Nothing is as important as nailing the big vision because often nothing at all will exist without it. Here, authenticity and growth are afterthoughts.

Most often, this phase accompanies the creation of some entirely new company, project, or effort. Acquiring the funding required to create a company from scratch demands a compelling vision. Even retirement requires a new, clear vision in order to pursue an authentic or growth approach.

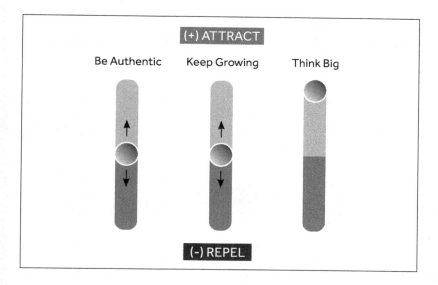

This phase is best when limited in duration because, while necessary at times, it is not fully Making It Yours. You might have a strong desire for action but be unable to take steps for lack of a clear goal. Lean into big thinking to stake out your territory and move forward.

SEASONED: ATTRACTIVELY YOURS

When you are authentic, growing, and thinking big, you are in the Seasoned phase. You know your team, and they know you.

While this is most often thought to happen after leaders and those around them have had time to form relationships, it happens more quickly for leaders who work hard at Make It Yours. You can even Make It Yours without anyone around you because it's all about being attractive. Those people light up with self-confidence—self-actualization—and it's incredibly attractive whenever it shows up.

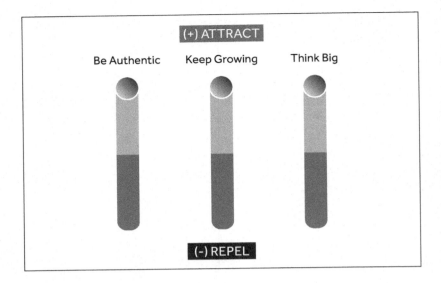

When you're here, keep stretching. Take a retreat with your team, create vision boards together, and accomplish meaningful stepping-stone goals. Ensure that your team is receiving some of the rewards they want most. Take one more class. Master one more skill. Nothing lasts forever, and you want to be sure that you and they look back on this time with joy. You are on fire, and it is awesome! This time should make you a better person and give them a better life. *This* is how you grow your network. *This* is how you get people in many places and roles who are ready to help, even when they no longer work with you. *This* is when, and how, you build a legacy that brings new opportunities, joy, and benefits for years to come.

START ATTRACTING

As you focus on Making It Yours, give yourself permission to loosen up. Authenticity, growth, and big thinking can be uncomfortable. Remember that this endeavor aims to attract stronger results for everyone.

Any efforts you make toward this goal already put your heart in the right place. And this is where your leadership and involvement can create the uniqueness that leads to great results. I think about James Corden, who added the unique Carpool Karaoke feature to his talk show simply because he can sing. One of my personal favorite examples of bringing lagniappe to a career is violinist Lindsey Stirling. Her shows and videos are more Broadway extravaganza than orchestra performance—and I love it.

When you really begin to Make It Yours, it shows up in your team's tremendous loyalty, tremendous commitment, and belief that being a part of your leadership journey is their best opportunity, one they don't want to miss. When you are in the Seasoned phase and really Making It Yours, be ready to feel the magic, and the responsibility, of being their unique leader. It is truly awesome.

A few years ago, my husband and I returned to LaPlace, Louisiana, where I'd been the bank's business development officer so many years earlier. We went back to our favorite fast-food restaurant, Frostop. The owner happened to be working there that day; he had been on the bank's board of directors nearly twenty-five years ago. After all those years, we hugged and swapped stories about what we had accomplished so many years ago. It was rewarding to realize that the job I had done in my own way had created new activities and new expectations for the bank. Adding my own lagniappe had *mattered*, and that felt so rewarding.

I don't know how it will work for you, but maybe one day you'll interview for just a job and walk out with a role you know you'll love.

Use Part 2 of the book to identify steps forward, and then add in some creativity!

Once you've Made It Yours, it's time to look around and give those around you that same permission to share their strengths and their weaknesses. It's time to Make It *Theirs*!

FIND YOUR PERSPECTIVE ON MAKING IT YOURS

The Start-Up
I wear ten different hats and am fighting to survive!

Before you opened your business, you hopefully studied your competition—its strengths and weaknesses. You probably identified your strengths and talents and why people would choose you or your product, rather than the competition. Making It Yours is your opportunity to bring your own passions and strengths into your business plan, so that you find your own niche, the specific market that **needs** you and your business."Bring your own passions and strengths into your business plan so that you find your own niche, the specific market that needs you and your business. Your team has chosen to dedicate themselves to your small business, so don't leave your skills, your personality, or your talents out of it. Let them shine, and the people who work with you will feel confident and comfortable in showing their strengths too.

The Freelancer
I'm on my own, but I still need good results!

This one should be a natural for you. As a freelancer, you have the ability to grow and learn in the areas that interest you most. Lead with the skills and talents that you enjoy the most. As a freelancer, live it up and Make It Yours!

The CEO
I feel responsible for everything!

Don't forget the ongoing value of being a great teacher. How can you communicate with a group of people, rather than one to one, and still let them feel your investment in their growth? How can you demonstrate that you are staying fresh and relevant to their success? Teaching is a great answer.

The New Manager
I was good at my job, but now how do I lead people?

This is your moment, and your way, to make your new leadership position matter. You don't want or need to change how everything is done, but adding in your own strengths and talents will remind people that a new leader has arrived and intends to make a difference.

The Virtual Leader
Virtual should not equal remote.

Virtual meetings have created an interesting look into the lives and homes of others. Late night hosts have introduced the world to the dogs and their spouses. Don't shy away from being you, or from being personal, even in a virtual setting. In fact it can be easier! Lean into the opportunity to share your personal environment, or if that is not possible, lean into choosing virtual settings that mean something to you, or to the mission. Continue to let your strengths and talents and personal qualities build trust with your team.

The Middle Manager
How do I matter with so many people above me?

This is one of the most important principles for you as a middle manager. How can you be a bit unique? Why does it matter that you are in this role instead of Bob or Susie down the hall? Start by being willing to share your talents and your genuine self with those you work with. Volunteer those same talents with a committee or a project that does not necessarily fit your daily role. Your unique talents and abilities can help you shine.

The Project Manager
I don't have anyone reporting to me!

There is a job to be done, but as the project manager, you probably have the freedom to do it in your own way and to add in your own perspectives. What must be done should be crystal clear, but the how may allow for freedom and personal input. Make It Yours!

Make It Yours vs. The Parked Pig

MAKE IT **THEIRS**

I t is a privilege and a joy to be a leadership coach. It is also a responsibility. As a coach of other leaders in the Keller Williams MAPS program, and now through my own coaching program, I have experienced the challenge of leading through listening, and of truly leading through others. These clients were creating their own leadership journeys, and it was my job to help them achieve success, however they defined it.

> *"People support a world they help to create."*
>
> — DALE CARNEGIE

In 2017, natural disasters were a theme in my work. I coached leaders all over the country, and Hurricane Harvey, Hurricane Irma, and the California wildfires were a reality for my coaching clients. In real estate, such events affect not only your family and friends, but also your ability to earn a living.

Then, in 2020, we faced a disaster of a different kind - COVID 19. This disaster became a unique coaching challenge, because the size of the disaster was not clear, the effects of the disaster were not clear and the end of the disaster was not clear. In other natural disasters, you could identify what had happened and what needed to be done to return to normalcy. The end was easily identifiable, even when not easy to achieve.

It was difficult to find a path in coaching during the aftermath. My clients wanted someone to talk to and someone to care about their pain because they needed to show strength most of the time. I also knew that they needed to take action, and help those they were leading take action, in order to lessen the impact and duration of the crisis.

"I don't know why we're bothering with a coaching call today," I heard. "I should have just canceled. It's awful here. I'm scared and overwhelmed, and I don't know if this office will be able to sell any houses at all anytime soon."

These first phrases told me that there was work to be done to make the call valuable. How could I help them lead when overwhelm was their biggest emotion? How could I coach them through their own fears and the fears of others?

I allowed a short time for emotion, and then asked, "If you could get people to help you do one thing today, what would that one thing be?" We focused on basic needs and corresponding actions. As I developed a structure for these types of coaching situations, the power of Make It Theirs became evident. First, the leaders focused outside of themselves, on what others could contribute and what others needed, and from that an action plan and next step unfolded. The leaders focused on the value of Make It Theirs and helping people find one positive step forward they could take today. Remembering to delegate not just tasks but also responsibilities instantly made things less overwhelming and more hopeful, more energetic. When leaders focused on what was within their control, they became less fearful. In giving control to others, leaders became more inspired and more inspiring. The more they could Make It Theirs, the more they could help others find their leadership, too.

In the virtual world, Making It Theirs is critical to keeping engagement high. Sitting at home and "watching" on zoom is too easy, turning off the camera to "listen" is too easy, and it creates distance even greater than the physical. Apathy, lethargy and a lack of caring more easily creep into a virtual world, and Make It Theirs can have a positive and energetic impact. A crisis can become an opportunity to create unity, to identify specific skills & talents, to be visible as a leader in your industry or in your community. A crisis can become a moment to serve, to help, to lead… and to be the ones who took action and moved forward. A moment to innovate and also persist. A moment to genuinely care.

In the aftermath of disaster, I saw how personal leadership needed to be, at every level of responsibility. However, genuine leadership cannot be about doing everything yourself. It's tempting, and maybe even satisfying, to get out there with your shovel and start clearing the streets. But someone must create the vision of the "new normal" as quickly as possible and then establish a long-term plan for a return to normalcy. There's nothing wrong with helping clear the streets, or handing out food packs. However to have the most impact, you'll also want to attract others to lead efforts to rebuild communication in a way that is effective right now, attract others to help with food or technology or cleaning…..and more. A disaster needs a plan, and a big plan needs a leader of leaders.

During this time, I rediscovered how important it is for attractive leaders to make what needs to be done something owned by and personal to those doing it. Attractive leaders will be open and honest about needing others, and those they need know it and feel it. In order to attract the best results, leaders engage the hands, heads, *and* hearts of those working with them. While that can be easier when a disaster strikes close to home, it is necessary with any leadership. A natural disaster or other major crisis is a crash course in the importance of the Make It Theirs principle because it is genuinely impossible to succeed alone.

Apply this principle to everyday leadership to be your most effective.

FOCUSING FACTS

- 96% of U.S. professionals say they need flexibility, but only 47% have it.[32]

- A lack of flexibility makes employees two times more likely to be dissatisfied at work.[33]

- 98% of marketers agree that personalization helps advance customer relationships.[34]

- Studies show that work motivation doesn't decline with age, it just shifts from prioritizing extrinsic rewards to intrinsic ones.[35]

- Autonomy is the number-one predictor of intrinsic (internal, self-driven) motivation.[36]

- Heinrich Anton de Bary coined the term *symbiosis* in 1879 as the living together of unlike organisms. What could be more unlike than a company and a person, a project and a person, or a team and a person? And yet each side of the pair needs the other half. There are three types of symbiotic relationships.

  ▷ Commensalism, when one of the pair benefits while the other simply tolerates (for example, a project or company benefits, but the individual does not).

32 Dean, Annie and Auerbach, Anna. "96% of U.S. Professionals Say They Need Flexibility, but Only 47% Have It." Harvard Business Review. Accessed: August 2020. https://hbr.org/2018/06/96-of-u-s-professionals-say-they-need-flexibility-but-only-47-have-it

33 Dean, Annie and Auerbach, Anna. "96% of U.S. Professionals Say They Need Flexibility, but Only 47% Have It." Harvard Business Review. Accessed: August 2020. https://hbr.org/2018/06/96-of-u-s-professionals-say-they-need-flexibility-but-only-47-have-it

34 Research International. Evergage, Inc. "2019 Trends in Personalization Survey Report." Accessed: August 2020. https://www.evergage.com/resources/ebooks/trends-in-personalization-survey-report/

35 Inceoglu, I., Segers, J., & Bartram, D (2012). Age-related differences in work motivation. Journal of Occupational and Organizational Psychology, 85(2), 300-329.

36 Patall E.A., Cooper H., Robinson J.C. The effects of choice on intrinsic motivation and related outcomes: A meta-analysis of research findings. Psychol. Bull. 2008;134:270–300. doi: 10.1037/0033-2909.134.2.270.

▷ Parasitism, when one of the pair benefits while the other is harmed (a project or company benefits, but the individual is harmed).

▷ Mutualism (also called reciprocal altruism), when both benefit (a project or company benefits, and the individual benefits)

WHAT IS MAKING IT THEIRS?

Imagine a Venn diagram in which two overlapping circles show how much you've succeeded in Making It Theirs. That overlap shows alignment between what you want, what they want, and what you both want. At its core, the overlap relies on being needed, and it also illustrates how much of their true self a person brings to the team and how invested they are in the outcome. When people believe they have an important contribution to make, they know that what they think or do matters.

Now imagine that whatever you're leading is so big—and such a perfect fit—that the people involved are all in. "All in" means they are fully themselves, fully accomplishing their own goals, and fully meeting their needs inside of your team, project, or company. It's hard to imagine, and it's easy to see that it's impossible to be all in if you don't feel needed.

So, what does it look like when you Make It Theirs? It looks like they're all in.

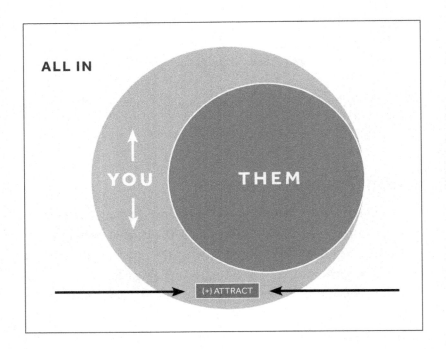

A Google employee had a visceral reaction to this illustration.

"I don't want Google to gobble me up!" he said. "Even if it is a great company!"

"Well," I asked. "What *would* it take for you to go all in? What dream world could exist?"

That question stumped him. Clearly Google hadn't asked it before. However, as we explored what it could look like, he outlined a scenario where he would go all in. Instead of working in ads, he'd write screenplays for YouTube original content. It wasn't related to his core role, and it probably wasn't possible. But that insight into what he loved and what needs were unmet revealed some steps that *were* possible to increase Google's attraction: a small related project, connections to people in the YouTube original content team, etc.

Google could do more to make it his, and our conversation showcased the potential result: energy, passion, happiness, ownership.

The all-in extreme isn't about achieving the end state. Instead, it's a challenge to increase the attraction. To Make It Theirs, you must be in a constant state of mutual benefit. Neither people nor projects are static, and Leadership by Attraction calls attention to the need to constantly expand and recalibrate how you Make It Theirs. If you don't, your overlap will decrease and eventually vanish.

In *Put Your Dream to the Test,* John Maxwell tells us that "the size of your dream determines the size of the people who will be attracted to it. If you have a very big dream, you have even greater potential for good people to help you. What you need to do is connect with them, invite them in, transfer the vision, and turn them loose." Your dreams must be big enough, far-reaching enough, that talented people can achieve their own dreams on the road to helping you achieve yours.

WANTED

THE PILE-IT-ON PIG

- Hangs around those who say,
  - ▷ "I can do it better."
  - ▷ "I can do it faster."
  - ▷ "I don't have [time, money, resources] to find someone else."

- Crimes:
  - ▷ Territorialism
  - ▷ Overly dominant attitude
  - ▷ Inability to see alternatives
  - ▷ Fear

Pile-It-On Pig annoys its neighbors and is wanted for trespassing. It digs where it's not wanted, claiming everything for itself. It's territorial, never seeing a task it shouldn't own. This pig snorts in your ear about what a mess it will be if you get someone else involved who doesn't do it as well—or as promptly—as you. Pile-It-On-Pig forces small thinking. It breathes fear: there's no time, or money, to get help anyway. Pile-It-On-Pig likes close pens with low ceilings, not wide-open spaces where the sky's the limit.

It can be both quicker and easier to just do things yourself. It is so very tempting to just add it to your responsibilities—even when it is a burden or barely possible to cram it into your schedule. Sometimes you even know that someone else could do it better, but you don't have that someone else or time to find them. Besides, they wouldn't do it *your way*.

Big goals and big visions require more than just you. Do you want to do something the best that you can do it or the best it can be done? In every situation, surrounding yourself with strong people grows the results and helps you achieve more. Surround yourself with people who don't wait for orders, who accept responsibilities not just tasks.

Leadership demands that your time, talent, and resources develop others. Make a plan to attract talent and then develop, educate, elevate, and trust the talent you attract. You must keep attracting and developing talented people even though it's time-consuming and even though people can disappoint you along the way. Yes, sometimes taking the steps to attract and develop true talent is downright scary.

Growing your team requires time and money, and it's scary and sometimes disappointing to seek true talent. In the face of those risks, it can feel necessary to take it on yourself. Here comes Pile-It-On Pig! It's squealing and snorting, "Just do it yourself!" It's rolling in the mud of not trusting others with the whole project or all of the results. Choosing not to invest in others makes you less attractive. People won't scramble to help or try to be a part of your world if you do all the awesome things by yourself, maybe leaving the scraps (generously, you might think) for someone else. People will look for other ways to spend their time and talent if you won't spend your time and talent to help them grow and achieve for themselves.

When you know delegation and trust are stuck, look around for Pile-It-On Pig!

WHY MAKING IT THEIRS ATTRACTS

The inspiration for Leadership by Attraction was the need to help leaders attract talent and results in a world that has changed dramatically and keeps reinventing itself. The moving target for attraction is driven by change.

In the midst of crisis, people embrace or reject change. When chaos reigns, is it about returning to the old life as quickly as possible? Or is the new outcome a silver lining? Have new unity, stronger relationships, new skills, or fresh perspectives emerged? Have new and improved tools and systems been developed? There are many quotes around the concept of nostalgia being a dirty seductive liar that paints yesterday as better than it actually was, and this can be a danger in the time following a crisis.

Coaching leaders in times of crisis taught me the importance of focusing on "felt needs." We need water and food, but people often felt a *need* to share the experience, to talk to others so they felt less alone. Leaders need to recognize that how people feel is frequently as important as facts and data. Focusing time and energy on felt needs, on giving people control over small steps, is the beginnings of Making It Theirs.

PEOPLE EXPECT IT

Commerce began one-on-one: eggs from my chicken traded for milk from your cow. Technology then allowed us to provide products and services from one to many: all the eggs sold to one store, and you go there to buy from them.

Today, technology allows us to provide products and services one-on-one again. I can get exactly the eggs I want, delivered exactly when and where I want them. Personalization is expected!

At some point, the people who came into contact with you as a leader were attracted. Perhaps it was only to a paycheck, but no one applies to a job without some attraction in effect. Making It Theirs is about making the job important and attractive for each individual. Know and understand why those around you chose this. Zoom in to see why each individual person shows up. Industrial and organizational psychologists study exactly this: what motivates individuals to come to work?

Broadly, people work to pursue positive incentives (for example, money, personal development, autonomy, a sense of purpose) and avoid negative incentives (demotion, being fired).[37] However, no one size truly fits all. An individual's motivation is complicated, connected to factors both personal (skills, background, relationships, microeconomics) and environmental (technology, culture, politics, macroeconomics). Anyone seeking to attract people is seeking to influence that individual's motivation to work.

PEOPLE NEED IT

Today, there is a lot of talk about the "loneliness epidemic." Single-person households are on the rise, technology allows someone to be social and alone simultaneously, and the rise in self-employment, remote work and side hustles means more people are working alone. None of these situations automatically create loneliness, but there is no doubt that people are searching for genuine connections. America's loneliness epidemic is getting worse, with three in five adults (61%) reporting they are lonely, a seven percentage-point increase from 2018, according to Cigna's 2020 Loneliness Index.[38] This stat is pre-pandemic, which will undoubtedly impact the loneliness epidemic in our country.

---

37 Deckers, L. (2010). *Motivation: Biological, Psychological and Environmental.* (3rd ed., pp. 2–3). Boston, MA: Pearson.

38 Cigna Takes Action To Combat The Rise of Loneliness and Improve Mental Wellness in America. Cigna Newsroom. https://www.cigna.com/newsroom/news-releases/2020/cigna-takes-action-to-combat-the-rise-of-loneliness-and-improve-mental-wellness-in-america

People need to feel needed. Knowing that your input, ideas, and participation matter creates a powerful tie to a group or project. Too many people feel that no one would notice if they just stayed home today, this week, this month. Too many people genuinely wonder whether anything would be different, or if anyone would care, if they just stayed in bed all day. But when you can harness someone's talent, you create retention, purpose, and a genuine desire to contribute at their highest level. When you make people feel needed, when you value their input and participation, they will stand beside you, work for you, and support you through many challenges. They will be your advocate when you aren't so fun or clear. This principle is central to you not only as a leader, but also as a member of humankind.

As a leader, you desire to work with people who are willing to give of themselves, their time, and their talents. To do that, you must value what they offer. You must recognize their contributions and reward their efforts. You must create an atmosphere where they can own the task, the responsibility, and the joy of being needed. When people feel like they matter to the project, the team, or the organization, they are attracted to the best results they can deliver and to the leader who made them feel that way.

So, is that all it means to Make It Theirs? Just make them feel needed? Well, yes and no. You need to give them ownership, connect them to the bigger vision, and encourage them to invest their best ideas and extra effort.

PEOPLE WANT IT

There are at least as many theories explaining individual motivation as there are psychologists studying it. Here's the gist:

- People are complicated. They work to fulfill the needs outlined in Maslow's hierarchy (food, water, security, relationships, achievement, self-actualization),[39] to maximize their return on investment in the workplace,[40] and to simply get satisfaction from the work itself.[41]

- In work life, Zig Ziglar identified a slightly different hierarchy of needs: safety, stability, success, and significance, in that order.

- By understanding and uncovering these needs, leaders can influence motivation to increase performance, boost likelihood of staying in the role, and generally get more out of any individual.

It's good news that leaders can influence motivation and attraction, but it isn't easy. It's complex, it's personal, and the need for it is never ending.

Making It Theirs requires intentional focus. Without focus, you'll be less attractive than you could be. There's just no way to accidentally maximize all the personal variables in motivation and attraction—it takes effort!

Try not to feel overwhelmed when thinking about knowing and influencing the personal motivations of those around you. Instead focus on attracting and retaining those who matter most, those who shape your own journey, and then count on them to Make It Theirs with others, too.

To start attracting, focus on what matters most to Make It Theirs.

---

39   Jex, S.M. & Britt, T.W. (2008). Organizational Psychology. Hoboke, New Jersey: John Wiley & Sons, Inc.

40   Lawler, E.E. & Jenkins, G.D. (1992). Strategic reward systems. In M.D. Dunnette and L.M. Hough (eds.), Handbook of industrial and organizational psychology (2nd ed., 1009–55). Palo Alto, CA: Consulting Psychologists Press.

41   Jex, S.M. & Britt, T.W. (2008). Organizational Psychology. Hoboken, New Jersey: John Wiley & Sons, Inc.

WHERE MAKING IT THEIRS ATTRACTS

You Make It Theirs when they own it and it's personal.

OWNERSHIP

Ownership is as simple as "I'm a part of this, and I'm going to be sure it succeeds!" It's normal and natural to get behind a decision or a plan when you're part of it. It is true that people only care about the color of the wall if they helped choose the color of the paint, helped pay for the new wallpaper, or celebrated the new look and feel of the room. They care about things they are a part of, things they contribute to, and situations where they feel they've had some control.

At its most basic, this is when you delegate not just the task but also the responsibility. You establish the what and allow contribution to the how. The most productive people seem to have the biggest struggle with delegating responsibility. Many high achievers have admitted to me that some days they long for someone to just do exactly what they tell them, but this is a limiting factor, not a growth factor. If no one can do anything that you haven't drawn out in detail already, then not much will get done when you are busy elsewhere. The success of your leadership is inversely related to your need to control the how.

When you hire the right who, it is a joy to let go of the how because you know it will be handled better than you could have done. This is an important piece of Making It Theirs. If the results will be inferior, you must take responsibility for having the wrong who, providing inadequate training for the how, or allowing a lack of clarity around the what.

Hesitating to hire someone who can achieve better results than you will limit your success. Once you've attracted the right talent, delegating the responsibility—not just the task—will get you superior results. And celebrating the successes of those who are choosing to go with you, to follow you, to support you is the sweetest celebration of all!

Ownership can also be found in connecting to a bigger vision. Knowing why you are doing what you are doing is a key for talented people. Belief in the why and permission to control the how is a powerful combination. How many times have you heard that people want to be part of something bigger than themselves?

As a volunteer, I have seen the power of this combination many times. In launching the Champions for Children Gala to benefit the Children's Advocacy Center for Denton County, I saw the absolute power of people embracing the why while also being allowed and expected to contribute to the how. Creating a major event can be overwhelming. However, when you attract the right people, it is entirely possible to get the right results!

Since there is much to be gained by sharing responsibility, it's worth facing these challenges head on. Leaders who attract will find ways to share ownership, to Make It *Theirs* instead of just yours.

WHY SHOULD I CARE?

Every Keller Williams office has a market center administrator (MCA), a CFO-type role, and because Keller Williams is a profit-sharing company, agents are invited to review office financials each month. It's boring, and the MCA is the only person who does it for a living. So, as you can imagine, our finance committee meetings were not well-attended.

As the leader, I decided that I should go. It was me, the MCA, and one other attendee.

"Oh no, Anne. Why are you here?" the MCA said, laughing, yet clearly sharing in the agents' dread. "Let's power through this."

It was clear that no one understood that individuals could shape the way the office ran, the services provided, and their own incomes by attending a finance committee meeting. It was a sign of disengagement from what really mattered.

I made it my mission to improve attendance, starting by asking all agents, "When we are the best real estate office in the world, how will we know?"

I made a poster where people could tack up photos of covered parking, fancy technology, increased staff, national speakers, and more. Homemade videos were sent to encourage the team to let me know what they really wanted. The front desk provided Atomic FireBall candies because we were on fire and wanted everyone's participation. It wasn't expensive, complicated, or time-consuming, and yet it became a buzz in the office, a different way to engage.

Someone finally asked, "What has to happen for the office to have some of these things?"

I answered, "There's a meeting where we make decisions on how we prioritize. We look at our budget and reports, just like you do for your own business. I'd love for you to check it out and share your perspective."

Others attended and learned where to find their own data within the KW systems. Then everyone participated in a lively debate about covered parking versus national speakers, and they all agreed on wanting a pellet ice machine.

It was a journey. And on the way, these agents fell in love with their office. They wanted to grow it and their own businesses to hit goals that were suddenly tangible. They became part of the office leadership and so were part of our shared success. It became personal when we budgeted for a national trainer, which led to great attendance at the event. And we celebrated the new ice machine!

At the finance committee meeting, they learned how to use their own reports and financial data to set and achieve priorities. It made a group into a team and helped the office take care of its people's priorities.

PERSONALIZATION

In scaling a business, you may have heard the phrase "I do it, we do it, they do it." The most important thing in scaling a business is the who." The right people make scaling possible, and the wrong ones make it impossible. So personalizing with and for the right talent is a must. If personalization is a desired outcome, then some flexibility is necessary. Can you create together something that fits and fulfills their needs?

Personalizing how people matter is not about losing focus on the business or project objective. Instead, it ensures that the objective has space for others' dreams. When your dreams and objectives keep growing, those who pursue them with you have room for continued personal growth too. To do this you must know the big stuff: what people want to do today, tomorrow, and in twenty years. These dreams are much bigger than the tasks and projects happening today.

Personalization also requires that future options be clear and available. People do not want their career or income stream to be managed randomly. They must understand their future options and see the education they'll need to embrace it. Bringing these things into focus for those who matter to you is a major attractor. People crave the right experience at the right time—and they'll work happily when they find it.

Imagine stepping up and down a staircase. As you move up and down the stairs, you can see different things. As you go up, you can still see what you saw before, but you also see a much bigger area with many more people, features, and opportunities. When you go down, you can see more details and intricacies. So, what are the people working with you seeing? When will what they see change and grow? Are you providing the big picture—or the granular view—they are looking for?

Connecting your objectives and plans to the individual dreams and hopes of those most important to your success will attract their contributions. As for recognizing their contributions and showing gratitude for their participation—well, that's when you earn their loyalty and trust, encourage their extra efforts, and find that the biggest results are possible.

REPELLENT: COMPLACENCY

Complacency, routine, boredom. Who wants that every day? And yet, ironically, strong capabilities and confidence in a role can create them. Someone—you or your team member—is most at risk for complacency when at their very best. Optimal work can be a small step toward complacency. Watch for it!

Complacency can show up in many different ways:

- **Blind spots:** something you did not know to look for or something different than what has happened before that leads to disruption. Blind spots let new strategies, or new hazards, slip by unnoticed.

- **Slowed pace:** a lack of urgency in producing achievable results. Slowdowns may produce poorer or fewer results, and they change the overall atmosphere and attitude as well. A slower pace eventually leads to missed deadlines and broken promises.

- **Change in feedback:** a change in how actively results are monitored or tracked along the way, a change in the amount of detail being discussed, or how frequently feedback sessions are missed or delayed. Don't be overconfident in results.

- **Attendance:** a change in how many events are missed, days taken off, or appointments delayed. If they've "got this," then why does a workday, meeting, or appointment really matter?

Repairing attraction requires an awareness of common signs of repelling and willingness to have those one-on-one conversations to find out whose needs are not being met and how to move forward. How can you boost personalization or grow your dream? How can you share more ownership?

KNOW WHERE YOU ARE

How much have you Made It Theirs? There are infinite gradients to ownership and personalization. However, there are a finite number of trends. There is a resting, typical level of engagement, and from there you can move toward or away from each other.

Part 2 of this book will help you assess where you are with Making It Theirs and start being more attractive. You can take simple steps today to understand and motivate with ownership and personalization. New project? New role? New company? Feeling stagnant? Feeling overwhelmed? Understand the options and see where you are with Making It Theirs.

TYPICAL

Let's return to the Venn diagram. Think about a typical relationship between leaders and the people they're leading. People are involved in their work because they find some elements enjoyable or aligned with where they want to go. In other words, most team members likely have some ownership and personalization, even unintentionally.

Ownership and personalization may take the form of a nice paycheck that facilitates "real life," or maybe some part of the job energizes them, or maybe your mission resonates with their self-identification. Many nonprofit organizations attract talent in this last way, leveraging a philanthropic mission to hire talented people who value similar things. Still, the work itself may be boring, the paycheck may be too small, or some other factor may keep overlap minimal.

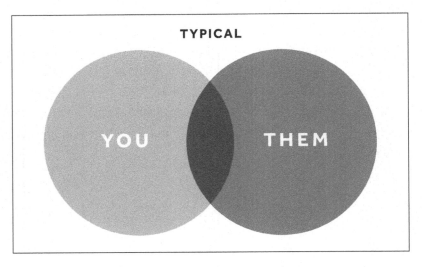

While typical is a common state, it's not exactly attractive. Leadership by Attraction seeks to increase the magnetism between you and them. Make It Theirs by increasing ownership and personalization to increase the overlap.

REPELLING: INCOMPATIBLE

When you and your team are on different pages, you are incompatible. Repelling positions are most common when there are clear incompatibilities between the leader's world and others'.

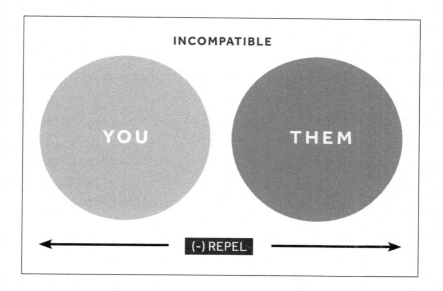

You need to know when things are incompatible because it is not a state of rest. Damage is being done as you and the others actively repel each other. Here's what may be going unsaid:

- Decreased Ownership: "I don't matter." "Why am I doing this?" "Why does it have to be done this way?" "Any idiot could do this."

- Decreased Personalization: "I can't grow here." "I'm not learning anything new." "I don't care about this." "I'm bored."

When companies, projects, or objectives shift, it can be hard for people who feel attached to the way things used to be. This is natural and healthy, and it may even lead to a mutual understanding that it's time for someone to move on.

Unrecognized incompatibility does the real harm. When team members or leaders change direction without sharing, for example, it feels like dissonance. Why did relationships change? What's suddenly slowed down—or worsened—performance? One big cause of unrecognized incompatibility is complacency. Someone complacent about the way something used to be (the old leader, the old mission, the old objective) may not even realize they're incompatible with the new world.

LOST

When you're lost, you're chasing the people around you. The lost leader thinks, "I'm busy and thankful for the help, any help. Please don't leave." It's a natural state in high-growth companies, where goals chase the people around them.

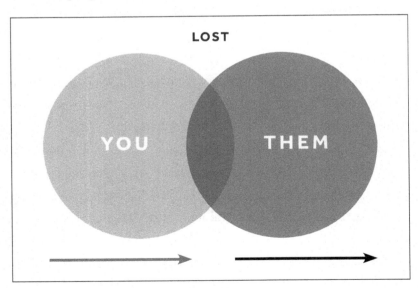

Tech-startup leaders in Silicon Valley often end up chasing others. With a culture of scrappy iterations and pivots, it can be easy to forget the original dream in the face of the latest feature or capability request. Combine that with an ultra competitive battle for talent, and it's not uncommon to see perks like free food and loose working environments accompanied by too much time and resources aimed at employee retention. Before you go buying a ping-pong table to retain your people, consider whether you are letting them own their tasks and processes, and how you show them they matter.

I have laughed through the years about T-shirts that read, "I am their leader, which way did they go?" In Leadership by Attraction, chasing those who should be following is not ideal. Those on your team and in your sphere need to be working with you toward a shared goal. They need to know their contribution to and role in achieving that goal, and they should value your contributions and leadership, too. The lost state can occur when people feel like they need to achieve around you or without you. Maximizing ownership and personalization maintains an overlap even in rapidly changing environments.

CHASING

In this situation, the team is constantly chasing someone who states, "I'm the leader. Follow or not. I don't really care." Unless you're working toward an intentional changing of the guard, having people chase the leader is bad. Wider company processes and cultural aspects may save you for a while, but eventually your team is going to get tired and leave. This is why even companies listed as the best places to work have areas with attrition problems.[42]

------

42   Hess, Abigail. "The 10 best places to work in 2019 , according to Glassdoor." Accessed: August 2020. https://www.cnbc.com/2018/12/04/glassdoor-the-best-places-to-work-in-2019.html

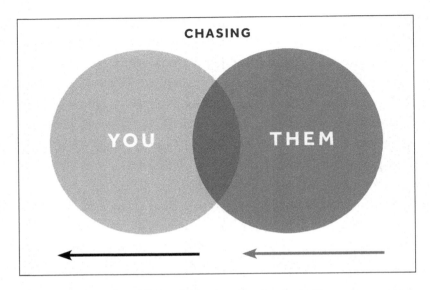

The driving force behind chasing is a leader's disengagement. A leader who makes no effort to share ownership or make it personal to those around them will repel talent. There may be a lot going on, but it's worth taking time to learn about and consider the dreams of the people around you. This can creep up on a busy leader, who may already feel like they are working as hard as they can. But when busy leaders thinks there's no time for the extra communication required to delegate responsibility or to personalize a plan, they enter a danger zone. Making It Theirs is a core principle for getting and *keeping* talent.

When times are good, a lack of connection or performance can be hidden by strong results. However, when challenges arise, you want to have people truly on your team and not chasing along, wondering what you're doing and why they are there. Author Susan Scott, in *Fierce Conversations*, points out that the gap between people is rarely the result of a failed conversation; instead, it is usually the result of a missing conversation. How can you have enough conversations? Can you have the right conversation enough times to take the right people with you?

ATTRACTIVE MATTERING

This is when both sides are moving closer together. You know what makes them tick, and they actively take more responsibility and tackle new challenges. Everyone is getting what they want, which is why this is the best spot. Leaders are attracting the people around them based on shared ownership and personalization.

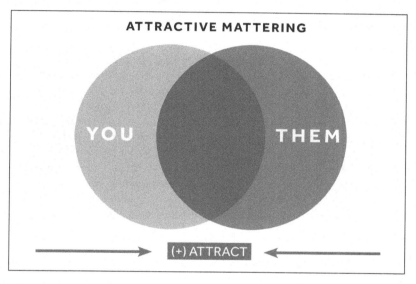

START ATTRACTING

People want to know what's in it for them. They want to know they're not wasting the hours they spend at work or on a project. They want confirmation that they matter, challenge in growth opportunities, and alignment with where things are heading at a personal level. As a leader, coaching others to produce better results that they own and better lives that they earned will win you loyal fans. You never know what disasters may strike, and sometimes the challenges of the day can feel like hurricanes, wildfires or pandemics, so get ready with empathy and strength to lead through whatever comes your way.

Harness the power of ownership and personalization to Make It Theirs and attract the right people. Head to the back of the book to get started!

FIND YOUR PERSPECTIVE ON MAKE IT THEIRS

The Start-Up
I wear ten different hats and am fighting to survive!

Realize that your strongest team members, and those investing their time in your journey, are trusting you to grow, and to allow them to grow as well. Keep trusting them, keep pushing them, and keep allowing them to learn; you may even reach the point of allowing them to hire their own assistants. That is an exciting time for any small business! And when someone sends you a referral, make sure you let them know when that referral is complete and that the referral is happy with your services. Let them feel ownership and pride because their referral received great service! You feel great when you help someone else, and so it makes sense that people feel great when they help your business too. As a small business, you want your team members, vendors, and referral givers to feel valued and important in your journey!

The Freelancer
I'm on my own, but I still need good results!

Make sure you give them what they are expecting—and more. When you are hired, make sure that you are prepared and capable of delivering the results they expect. And give credit where credit is due: to those who welcomed you into the role, even for a short term, or who provided services to you so that you could do your best work. Show appreciation and inclusiveness, letting them be a part of your journey to the next assignment.

The CEO
I feel responsible for everything!

Your direct reports and your inner circle—are you hearing from each of them? Do both know that you need them and count on them? Make sure that communication channels to your inner circle remain open so they know what you need and have the opportunity to get it for you. They have already raised their hands and told you that they want to be a part of your success, so make sure your schedule and your direct line allow them to connect!

The New Manager
I was good at my job, but now how do I lead people?

Sharing ownership is an important step in creating a trusting, communicative team. Remember that a group is people gathered together, but a team requires shared purpose and shared experiences. Find tasks, times, and ways to trust and delegate, and set clear expectations for them. It's okay to start small and see who earns the bigger delegations. It can be tempting to hold tightly to all tasks until you know people better.   However be intentional about Making It Theirs, or you will remain a group rather than a team and your productivity will suffer.

The Virtual Leader
Virtual should not equal remote.

Make It Theirs is the secret sauce for a virtual leader! It retains talent, interest, engagement and effort by sharing responsibilities, sharing the stage. When leading virtually, it can be too easy to talk at people, rather than with people. You ask a zoom room for input and frequently the response is silence. Maybe they're on mute, maybe their internet is poor.....a few meetings in this environment and getting people to bring their best talents and efforts to your project will become even more challenging. Be intentional. Delegate small duties and big responsibilities. Let people know you need them to share their findings, share their planned next steps. It matters to you if they are with you or not - so make sure you say that clearly and allow them to feel it as they lead too.

The Middle Manager
How do I matter with so many people above me?

Your ability to tell your story is important here. Where are you going, and how are they (and what they are doing) going to help you get there? You feel like a middle manager, but to them, you are their coach, their dream-giver, and their vehicle to get where they want to go. So include them, give them feedback on why what they did today had impact, and keep telling the story of where you are all going together.

The Project Manager
I don't have anyone reporting to me!

Seek out people working on similar projects, relevant projects, or projects that may connect with yours at some point. Share your progress with them and check in on their progress. You are all working toward a greater goal, so make sure they know you value what they are doing. While collaboration may not be necessary or even appropriate, acknowledgment and communication can create relationships and trust. Relationships and trust lead to more exciting projects and inclusion in more exciting initiatives. Islands can be pleasant, but remember that it takes intention and effort to connect them with others.

Make It Theirs vs. The Pile-It-On Pig

....

....

....

....

....

....

....

....

....

....

....

....

....

....

....

....

....

....

....

MAKE IT **HAPPEN**

Leadership by Attraction is not a philosophy for contemplation. It is all about action. Each of the principles leads to actions that increase your attraction. However, this final principle is all about action.

My husband worked in the wine business for years. As sales manager for an Orlando wine distributor, he occasionally worked with suppliers to schedule in-store demos. It wasn't something we talked or even though about; it was unremarkable marketing.

> *"Thoughts do more. Words do much. Actions do much more."*
>
> — ISRAELMORE AYIVOR

Then, on the Saturday before Christmas, one of the biggest retail accounts called to say that he'd asked the demonstrator to leave his store. Why this happened didn't matter. Extra product had been ordered, and even though we both would have loved that day off, Mike chose to Make It Happen. He handled the demo himself to soothe the store manager and sell some product. In fact, five times as much product as had ever been sold in a three-hour demo.

We wondered why. What had Mike done that was so different, so much better than the normal wine tasting? Could others be trained to do what he did? We decided that, yes, with some simple steps, demonstrators could be more successful at sales. Again, we Made It Happen and created Taste of Orlando, a food product demonstration company. For two years, Taste of Orlando did demonstrations across the state of Florida for alcoholic beverage companies, Frito Lay, Nestlé Foods, and many others. It took us to Daytona for biker week, where I met amazing people while arranging product demos!

In this niche, no one had taken the time to be clear about the desired result: not just handing out samples, but actually selling product. Samples were a cost to make sales happen, so we focused on that as the goal. We encouraged and expected creativity in setting up the display, but we insisted on standards like logoed aprons, trash cans to keep the area clean, and most importantly, placing the product in the customer's hands so they could touch it, feel it, and buy it.

When we decided to take action and Make It Happen, we had no idea where it would lead. This is the power of momentum. Taste of Orlando started with alcoholic beverage companies—where we had relationships—but after it gained energy, other consumer product companies came calling. Once things get going, your systems start improving, your voice gains confidence, your smile becomes powerful, and momentum keeps you going. There's no need for a more complicated definition because it's just that feeling of things getting easier.

Think about a sports team when all the shots are going in or a run of winning days. Real estate agents are frequently told to leave a closing and immediately make calls to new leads—the momentum will give them a better tone and more energy to turn that lead into a client.

Nike's *Just Do It* slogan, which celebrated its thirtieth anniversary in 2018, is now a part of culture. It feels empowering to throw caution to the wind and just take action. "Analysis paralysis" has many people longing to make bold decisions, and Nike's slogan appeals to the innate desire to Make It Happen. The Just Do It campaign made Nike a unique icon in both sports and fashion, and it has attained huge retail success since that first ad in 1988.

As a leader, people look to you for decisiveness. If you take too long to make decisions, or avoid making them all together, you handicap your effectiveness and limit the success of the team.

Norman Vincent Peale said, "Action is a great restorer and builder of confidence. Inaction is not only the result, but the cause, of fear. Perhaps the action you take will be successful; perhaps different action or adjustments will have to follow. But any action is better than no action at all."

> *"Action is the foundational key to all success."*
>
> — PABLO PICASSO

Herminia Ibarra's book *Act Like a Leader, Think Like a Leader* states that "the only way to think like a leader is to first act: to plunge yourself into new projects and activities, interact with very different kinds of people, and experiment with unfamiliar ways of getting things done… In times of transition and uncertainty, thinking and introspection should follow action and experimentation—not vice versa."[43]

Every day, leaders must try to Make It Happen in the right direction, toward the desired outcome.

---

43 Ibarra, Hermina. "Act Like a Leader, Think Like a Leader." Excerpt Accessed: August 2020. https://herminiaibarra.com/act-like-a-leader-think-like-a-leader-european-business-review/

FOCUSING FACTS

- Job seekers who are currently employed listed boredom as the top reason they are looking for a new job.[44]

- After adjusting for inflation, the last-ranked company in the Fortune 500 is nearly five times bigger in terms of revenue than it was in 1990.[45]

- 60% of employees must consult with at least 10 colleagues each day just to get their jobs done. Scarier, half of them need to engage more than 20 others to do their work, based on responses from a workplace survey of more than 23,000 employees.[46]

WHAT IS MAKING IT HAPPEN?

When it comes to taking action, there's a lot of conflicting advice on what makes a leader successful. Proposals include:

- Act the fastest. Leaders hear about a program, think about an idea, and commit to something; as they leave a meeting, they're already making calls to take action.

- Steady the ship. Leaders embody the adage "slow and steady wins the race." After all, getting things done is a matter of persistence: keep trying in small iterations until something works.

---

44 Breaking Boredom: Job Seekers Jumping Ship for New Challenges in 2018. Accessed: August 2020. https://www.kornferry.com/press/breaking-boredom-job-seekers-jumping-ship-for-new-challenges-in-2018-according-to-korn-ferry-survey

45 Monahan, Tim. The Hard Evidence: Business is Slowing Down. Accessed: August 2020. http://fortune.com/2016/01/28/business-decision-making-project-management/

46 Monahan, Tim. The Hard Evidence: Business is Slowing Down. Accessed: August 2020. http://fortune.com/2016/01/28/business-decision-making-project-management/

- Set the tone. Leaders concentrate on how they show up each day in order to create an environment of successful action for others, rather than taking action themselves.

What about a combination? An intention to make something good happen can lead to quick action and, if it's not successful, a quick pivot to some other action.

Make It Happen is a lens through which to judge an action's attractive qualities. This lens is made up of two things: speed and direction. Those who Make It Happen—who attract with their actions—are moving fast in the right direction.

FAILING WELL

One of the most common action blockers is fear: fear of failure, fear of a poor outcome, fear that your pride may get smashed. Have you ever told someone they're wrong? Been told you were wrong? Really flubbed a paper, or a performance, or any task?

Failing with class or grace of any sort was not a natural behavior for me. I do not have a history of handling it well. When I found out I'd lost the election for State House by a few votes, I was at my own victory party. Thankfully, I was able to focus on friends, gratitude and get through it with some sort of grace, but the moment I got home, I was mad. The first thing I did was use the voter registry to count the people who hadn't voted. I moped around the house. I avoided the grocery store because I couldn't bear the idea of receiving sympathy. I was embarrassed.

Thomas Edison said, "I didn't fail one thousand times. The light bulb was an invention with one thousand steps." Baloney. It sucks to fail. Failing feels worse than succeeding. I like to think Edison was pissed each time his light bulb blew up.

Still, attractive leaders know that failure is a momentary event, a step in the process. Attractive leaders know that if their dreams and goals are big enough, failure is a part of their future.

In looking back, it's easy for me to see that losing that election was in fact a blessing, and a step in my journey. I hope you find a way to rapidly see any "failures" this way too.

SPEED ALONE CANNOT MAKE IT HAPPEN

Speed is not synonymous with attraction. The world is speeding up: commuting now doubles as a chance to read the news, lunch breaks moonlight as social media catch-ups, and even going to the bathroom is a chance to squeeze in a Candy Crush level. But speed comes at a cost. Some get left behind, and a faster pace can indicate higher stress levels, which lead to health problems like heart attacks and burnout.[47] Prolonged stress actively blocks attraction. It blocks oxytocin, the hormone responsible for building relationships of trust and unity. You want oxytocin. Oxytocin is the hormone of attraction!

You need more than speed to Make It Happen.

DIRECTION ALONE CANNOT MAKE IT HAPPEN

A plan, no matter how good, cannot attract. A vision may draw in capital and people, but a dream alone is not attractive.

Comedian Amy Poehler sums up the feeling: "I want to be around people that do things. I don't want to be around people that talk about what other people do. I want to be around people that dream and support and do things."

There is an ocean between those who stop at ideas and those who turn them into reality. How many garages are full of partial inventions? Computers filled with notes for some future day? Success depends on your ability to Make It Happen because thinking and imagining alone don't accomplish anything. Maybe you do it yourself, or maybe you attract people who can make your ideas reality. Either way, success is based on the ability to Make It Happen, and that ability attracts others who want to Make It Happen, too.

---

47   Stress and Heart Health. Accessed: August 2020. http://www.heart.org/en/healthy-living/healthy-lifestyle/stress-management/stress-and-heart-health

As billionaire entrepreneur Wayne Huizenga puts it, "Some people dream of success, while other people get up every morning and make it happen." He certainly lived that sentence, founding or acquiring portions of AutoNation, Waste Management, Blockbuster Video, Boca Resorts, the NFL's Miami Dolphins, the NHL's Florida Panthers, and the Florida Marlins baseball team.

So, direction alone won't Make It Happen either.

REPELLENT: TOO MUCH DATA

Data makes you think, while emotion makes you act. What is a leader to do with all of the data that comes their way? *Big data* is big business today. An entire industry (Box, DropBox, Google Cloud, Amazon Web Services, etc.) now supports companies' growing need to measure and access information. Control of data, being "data-driven" is everything.

Good luck rationalizing action on a gut feeling! It's highly likely you'll be blocked by a boss, colleague, partner, or employee who's on the big-data bandwagon. That's not necessarily a bad thing, but it's also not necessarily a good thing.

The problem with the big-data fad is its paralyzing effect on decisions, which stems from a gap between the power of numbers and the ability to take action based on them. Everyone feels data leads to better decisions, and yet few know how to do it right.

A common manifestation of this blocker is imagining a chart that tells a story and then going on a journey to find numbers that make that chart a reality. Someone might say, "I've put a placeholder in our presentation for a chart going up and to the right. Can someone find the data to create it?" Here, a decision has already been made, and so the search for numbers just feeds the big-data black hole, delaying the action instead of informing it.

Attractive leaders know that numbers and data are important, but only when they help make decisions. The big-data black hole is analysis paralysis: there is no end to the things you could search for and review.

THE GOAL: FAST AND GOOD

Inertia says that a body at rest tends to stay at rest, but once it's moving it tends to keep moving. The change from rest to movement—or movement back to rest—requires an external force. It requires action. It requires something to Make It Happen. That's you. You've got to get things moving.

Once you're moving, see if what you're doing and where you're going are any good. Results are attractive. Accomplishments are attractive. And results attract others who desire success.

WHY MAKING IT HAPPEN ATTRACTS

Rosabeth Moss Kanter wrote, "Actions produce energy and momentum. It simply feels better to take action than sitting around."[48] There may be no more obvious—or more neglected—truth in leadership. Put simply, "something happening" is attractive.

In fact, your brain is hardwired for action. It's an organ designed to solve problems related to surviving in an unstable outdoor environment and to do so while in nearly constant motion.[49] Humans were not the strongest on the planet, but developing the strongest brains led to our survival.

Because this evolution occurred in conditions of constant motion, you might predict that the optimal environment for processing information would include motion. Indeed, research shows that the best meeting would have everyone walking at slightly less than two miles per hour. Research also found that cognitive scores in the elderly were

---

48 Kanter, Rosabeth Moss. "Four Reasons Any Action Is Better than None." March 2011. Harvard Business Review. https://hbr.org/2011/03/four-reasons-any-action-is-bet.html

49 Medina, John. Brain Rules. Accessed: August 2020. http://www.brainrules.net/exercise

positively, and profoundly, influenced by exercise. Your brain is at its best when you are in motion, undertaking action.[50]

There's a reason Facebook so famously started its business with the mantra "Move fast and break things." That mantra has since changed to a safer, Wall Street–friendly, big-company mantra, but by moving fast, Facebook attracted talent from slower, more corporate competition.

MAKING IT HAPPEN ATTRACTS

So, where do you need to be both fast *and* good? The trick to attraction is in the decisions that leaders make. Decisions are the source of action, and so they need to be fast and good.

Make It Happen in your decisions.

TWO PARTS TO EVERY DECISION

Checking for oncoming traffic before turning at an intersection is a fast decision in which the brain goes through two stages: process and decision.

The process is when relevant evidence is collected. What do you see in the other lanes? Are there stop lights or signs that signal safety? What about pedestrians in the road? Your brain focuses on the relevant and filters out the irrelevant—maybe there's someone selling hot dogs on the corner, but if they're not in the street it's unlikely you'll remember seeing them. Then comes the decision: your brain processes the information collected during the decision process and decides it's either safe or unsafe to make the turn.

When leading businesses, people, and projects, your brain works basically the same way. You go through the process and make the decision.

---

50   Medina, John. Brain Rules. Accessed: August 2020. http://www.brainrules.net/exercise

FAST PROCESS, PAUSED DECISIONS

For the process to be successful, the decision itself must be clear so that relevant information is gathered. What exactly is the challenge or the opportunity? What do you have to decide first?

Then assess. External analysis gathers the information, and internal analysis pulls in what you already know, how you feel, and your own experiences. Speed is important in the assessment process. Getting ready to get ready is not Leadership by Attraction. A range of information and solid data are important, but you will never know everything… and an overload of information can stop progress in its tracks.

Leaders who attract go through these first steps with speed and determination to quickly arrive at an understanding of the options. At the point of reviewing evidence and understanding alternatives, a pause is in order. The decision's scope, importance, and likely impact help determine the length of the pause. Use it to weigh plausibility and desirability, pros and the cons, the best possible outcomes and the worst. Columbia University found that postponing a decision by as little as fifty to one hundred milliseconds enables the brain to focus attention on the most relevant information and block out irrelevant distractions.[51] However, there's a big difference between a postponed decision and a prolonged process.

Leadership by Attraction demands a fast process and a paused decision. In fact, the speed of the world today requires the same. If your process is too long, or if you procrastinate on a decision, the data will change, the competition will change, everything will change.

Make It Happen with a fast process and a paused decision, not a

---

51   Teichert, Tobias; Grinband, Jack; Ferrera, Vincent. "The Importance of Decision Onset." Journal of Neurophysiology. Vol 115, Issue 2. Accessed: August 2020. https://journals.plos.org/plosone/article?id=10.1371/journal.pone.0089638

prolonged or procrastinated one. And don't underestimate the power of the pause! It allows you to inject energy and passion into the action, and that will create momentum.

KNOW WHERE YOU ARE

If you take one thing from this chapter, remember that you've got to *do something*. Leadership by Attraction aims for fast and good, but it settles for motion. When you're caught in inertia, only an external force—you—will get things going. Once you're moving, it's a lot easier to keep going and to change direction.

So, where are you with Making It Happen?

	SLOW	FAST
GOOD	SLOW & GOOD	FAST & GOOD (+) ATTRACT
BAD	SLOW & BAD (-) REPEL	FAST & BAD

REPELLING: SLOW AND BAD

There's work to be done. While it's unlikely you are slow and bad in every area of the project or company, remember where Making It Happen matters the most: your decisions. If you are making slow, bad decisions, or if you're unwilling to commit to an action, then you're repelling people and results. Introspect and act. Part 2 of the book is here to help.

BURNOUT: FAST AND BAD

You know you're here when the pace of change is blistering but the results and people aren't along for the ride. This is where employees often find themselves in burnout mode. People want to matter; they want results and accomplishments, but they can find themselves caught up in all the action. People cannot operate here for long.

SPEED IT UP: SLOW AND GOOD

This is most common for companies or projects that are still attached to the way things used to be. It's the team that gets good results but is distracted by the swirl above or around it. It's the company struggling to keep up with consumer changes. The company that just isn't sure, or the leader who wants just a bit more intel before deciding. Their results may still be good, but things are slow, change is slow and the clock is ticking. You're not attracting the best talent for the best results.

ATTRACTIVE: FAST AND GOOD

This is it. Recognizable in the energy of action and the fulfillment of results, fast and good is not just addictive, it is exponential. This state benefits from momentum in that the movement continues. So, be vigilant! Watch for bureaucracy or red tape, often disguised as optimization, that slow things down. Watch for threats to your direction and signals that changes may be necessary.

START ATTRACTING

Make It Happen is the most important part of Leadership by Attraction because without it, all you've got is words on paper, ideas in your head, good intentions without results. Make It Happen serves a dual purpose as both its own principle—How much do you Make It Happen? How can you boost attraction by Making It Happen?—and a wider Leadership by Attraction mantra: get after it!

Put simply, you can't attract people and results if you don't Make It Happen. If you never act with urgency, you will be too slow and too boring and too behind. How can you make a product sampling (or whatever task is in front of you today) five times better? Can you "bottle" your ideas into something creative and urgent, something that you and others can implement today? Can you make something disruptive and industry-changing happen? We were able to sell Taste of Orlando because we helped disrupt an industry.

Think of Make It Happen as a call to action for Leadership by Attraction, and check out Part 2 to consider where your action will have the biggest return. Make It Happen by understanding which of the five Leadership by Attraction principles needs your attention first in the Personal Diagnostic.

So, read on! The next part of this book will help you assess the best place to start Making It Happen!

FIND YOUR PERSPECTIVE ON MAKING IT HAPPEN

The Start-Up
I wear ten different hats and am fighting to survive!

Be obvious about the fact that you are Making It Happen. As a small start-up company, a lack of achievement or progress can be scary for your employees, your vendors, your family. So, when you Make It Happen—when action is in progress—be sure to share, loudly and frequently. As a small business owner, you are defying the odds. You are creating your own future, the future of your employees and your family—you are Making It Happen! So many people talk about owning their own business, but few succeed in starting and even fewer last. Talk about that openly, and don't underestimate the potential of your business.

The Freelancer
I'm on my own, but I still need good results!

Freelancing can mean flexibility and freedom. However, it's easy to have so much freedom and flexibility that you never actually Make It

Happen. You never get enough work to earn sufficient income or build the reputation you imagined. No matter where you are in your freelance journey, it's good to figure out how to dedicate a part of each day, or each week, for revenue generation. Even if you have a project in hand, don't get so caught up in the now that you forget about generating a project for tomorrow.

The CEO
I feel responsible for everything!

Identifying the decision or direction is an important role for you as the CEO. Even more important, however, is how you share the decision or direction. Slow down and clearly express the importance of the actions that will happen or have happened to get you there. When a company feels stale, slow, or out-of-touch, it means that you as the CEO are not Making It Happen or that it's happening and you're not sharing it often enough or in the right ways.

The New Manager
I was good at my job, but now how do I lead people?

Be purposeful in the actions you take each day because people are watching to see if you matter to the role you have just assumed. You probably don't need to change everything, but be sure that you are doing something. What's something that happened this week that people want or need to know? Did you create it, ask for input around it, tweak it, lead it, encourage it, stop it, start it, slow it down, celebrate it? Tell your team and your boss about it so they can begin to know you and the way you work, the things you value. Tell them so they will know you are already Making It Happen.

The Virtual Leader
Virtual should not equal remote.

The virtual leader must check in around the 4 principles the most often! When working remotely, the focus on results must be at its strongest and the identification of the "pigs" that are derailing progress must happen as soon as possible. The inherent flexibility of virtual work can be both an attractor and a detractor. Many are attracted to the concept of flexibility and it is up to the leader to attract the results while embracing that flexibility. This requires intentionality and open-ness. Constant reminders of the big vision and how the individual's contributions matter to results.

The Middle Manager
How do I matter with so many people above me?

Your opportunity to make an impact will probably come in speeding up the process of gathering information and developing options. Make sure that each person around you knows exactly what information is relevant and what may not be relevant. Ensure that each person knows how and what info to gather quickly. Make speeding up the process your domain!

The Project Manager
I don't have anyone reporting to me!

Understand where your project fits into the whole and its importance. Is it an early-stage project or a finish-line project? Are you clear on the reason for the project, its placement, any timelines? Make sure that you communicate frequently with anyone you are depending on and anyone depending on you. Don't allow stress to creep in because you have forgotten to share your expectations about what you need from others or to share your absolute commitment to Making It Happen. Anything less will mean that your next project will be less important... or won't arrive at all.

TAKE ACTION

You've read the book. Now it's time to use it!

Part 2 of Leadership by Attraction is meant to be used over and over again. New project? New role? New company? Feeling stagnant? Feeling overwhelmed? This section will help you assess your current position and then provide actionable steps toward becoming more attractive. It includes general assessments and activities to help you apply Leadership by Attraction and Pass Your Pig.

This is the fun part. Reading about principles is nice, but putting them to work will instantly reveal the difference attraction can make, no matter your leadership position. Good luck, and enjoy your journey of Leadership by Attraction!

LEADERSHIP BY ATTRACTION
PERSONAL DIAGNOSTIC

This personal review will help identify where you are and which areas need your attention first. You may also visit *passthepigbook.com* or *leadershipbyattraction.com* and complete this diagnostic online. This tool can produce a general review of your role in a company, nonprofit, family, project, or other endeavor. It will also work for specific challenges, such as meeting attendance down, too many mistakes, sales slowing, donations not meeting goal.

Name the role, project, challenge, opportunity, mission, problem, or issue to be analyzed. Then, use the scale below in answering the questions and statements that follow. Be honest! In each challenge you analyze, where are you *really*? How are you participating in that challenge right now?

1. **No intentional action.** This is not a priority, or I lack confidence in taking action.
2. **Occasional action.** This area is not a strength, and my intention/effort is spotty.
3. **Purposeful action.** I'm aware of successes/failures here, taking planned action and measuring results.
4. **This is a priority.** I rely on this strength and use it in day-to-day leadership.

Take the Quiz!

	Your Score 1-4
MAKE IT CLEAR	
1 I have direct, purposeful conversations when needed. I schedule and prepare for these conversations rather than avoiding them.	
2 I have a written plan for keeping my strengths current and my knowledge fresh.	
3 I understand the difference between urgent and important, and I actively use that to focus my time.	
4 I have quality standards. People know my quality standards and when quality matters most.	
5 My responses and workflow are steady, strong, and dependable. People know they can rely on me, my work patterns, and my reactions.	
6 I am passionate and excited about what I am doing, and everyone knows it.	
7 I know the big vision, and so do the people most important to achieving it.	
8 I know the next steps and first milestone goals. The most important people know them too.	
9 I communicate through a variety of methods so that people with diverse styles receive the information.	
10 I know how success is measured—what it looks and feels like.	

MAKE IT FUN	
1	There is a plan for the next celebration, including a budget and leadership.	
2	I encourage small, spontaneous celebrations or fun conversations.	
3	I have a budget and goals for fun. I ask about fun, expect fun, and show appreciation for fun.	
4	I am aware of when and how often I should attend fun.	
5	Productivity is valued, and buzz is created around it. We are great at what we do.	
6	There are times, places, and opportunities for casual conversations, socializing, and catching up.	
7	I bring high energy and enthusiasm to the most important things.	
8	We have a learning event, or contest, that is fun, different, outdoors, or offsite planned and on the calendar.	
9	The work environment is updated regularly to ensure that it is energizing, bright, easy to use, fresh.	
10	Creativity and brainstorming are encouraged and calendared (for myself as well as others).	

MAKE IT YOURS	
1	I have the skills necessary to lead, or I have a schedule and plan to acquire the skills needed.	
2	I have identified my biggest strength(s) as related to this role.	
3	I know of two ways in which I am unique and different in this role.	

4	I am excited about what could be next for me—my next twelve months and my next three years.	
5	I know which pieces of what I am doing today will help me get to my desired next step.	
6	I am challenged by the role and feel stretched or uncomfortable regularly.	
7	I have a written education/training plan for myself for this month and this year. I encourage those around me to have one too.	
8	I share my talents, hobbies, or passions in ways that inspire and educate others.	
9	I have identified my biggest weakness(es) as related to this role.	
10	I read books related to my role, the big vision, and success strategies. So do the people around me, because sharing is valued..	

MAKE IT THEIRS

1	Key members of my team know the value of their contributions.	
2	I say thank you and show gratitude each day, each week, each month. I am specific.	
3	I participate in establishing the goal for what. The how belongs to others. I do not direct each step.	
4	I ensure that recognition is frequent and empowering.	
5	I know who my most important people are, including those I haven't yet attracted.	
6	I have a plan and a schedule for one-on-one conversations with key people.	
7	I am confident in my guided conversation/ coaching skills and in my ability to have effective conversations.	

8	I am comfortable delegating responsibilities. I do not need to know every detail, every day. I give credit to others regularly.	
9	I know the strengths, weaknesses, and goals of my key team members.	
10	I am intentional about listening.	
MAKE IT HAPPEN		
1	I have resources to find answers and get help quickly and with confidence. I know I will need help.	
2	I create a vision of success with ease. I can tell you how we will know when we succeed at next steps and larger goals.	
3	I embrace change. I know the steps of awareness, understanding, adoption, and implementation. I move comfortably from one step into the next.	
4	I work with urgency and expect urgency in those around me. I thrive on a fast pace in most situations.	
5	I respond to setbacks with calmness, flexibility, determination, and speed. I respond to disappointment with curiosity first.	
6	Our steps, our goals, and our big vision have timelines and deadlines.	
7	I encourage key people (including myself) to admit errors and oversights openly. We look for answers and improvements rather than stress and shaming. Honest status reviews and updates are expected and scheduled.	
8	I take and encourage appropriate risks but not recklessness. We understand, and openly discuss.	
9	I am not surprised by our results. I stay up to date on progress and trends to make adjustments along the way.	
10	There is a job description and a succession plan to encourage consistency and collaboration. If I'm not here (or they're not), we know what should happen.	

Now that you've rated yourself on each specific statement, average those scores to get your overall score for each principle.

If you have an average of 3 or better in one of the categories, it is a strength area for you (green). If you have an average of 2 or less in one of the categories, that area requires your focus (red). Areas averaging between 2 and 3 are on your mind but not a strength zone (yellow); in these areas you are not truly attracting the right people and the right talent to achieve your goals.

Use these scores to get real and get specific! Once you have identified your personal challenges, find that principle in the exercises below.

Your results will change depending on your situation and what you're analyzing: is it a specific project, a charity leadership role, a family project, or your performance within an entire industry?

It's not true that you either are a leader or you aren't. Leadership ebbs and flows depending on the moment. The goal is to be mindful of the need to attract so that you can find the right people and produce the right results in more areas, with more ease, and more frequently throughout your life. Don't you want that?

RELATIVE **ATTRACTION**

Leadership by Attraction focuses on specific areas to attract the right people and drive the right results. Maximizing attraction is the key, and yet, theoretically, the pursuit of maximization could be unending. This is where you must remember that attraction is relative.

Thank goodness for this relativity! Attraction's relativity ensures that the effort put into Leadership by Attraction is grounded in reality, avoiding lofty, exhaustive lists that no leader could ever keep up with. To attract your people, you must only out-attract the other things pulling at them.

For example:

- You don't have to be crystal clear all the time. You just need to be more clear than expected, more clear than your competition, and more clear than the alternative.

- Work doesn't have to be fun all the time. It just needs to be more fun than the alternative and fun often enough to keep people energized.

The time has come for the inevitable magnet analogy. Imagine two U-shaped magnets on opposite sides of a table, competing to attract a pile of metal marbles at the table's center. One of the magnets is you (your project, your business, etc.). The other magnet is your competition for the talent you need. The metal marbles in the center are the people you want.

As your magnet comes closer to the marbles, they are attracted to it. Your products, your leadership, your company culture, your pay, your growth opportunities, your brand—all of them work to attract the people you need to get the results you want.

However, as the competitive magnet gets closer, some of the marbles will be attracted to it. If that magnet is much more powerful than yours, it could attract the lion's share of the marbles, sometimes even ripping those that were firmly stuck to your magnet right back across the table.

However, you don't need the world's strongest magnet to attract the marbles available in the middle of the table. Attraction is relative. You just need a force more powerful than that of the competition.

Who else is attracting your people and thus your results? Your competition is anyone whose attraction competes with your own.

- If you sell ice cream from an ice cream truck,
  - ▷ Competition for people is anything that absorbs the time and talent of your potential employees. For example, it may be local part-time employment, like lifeguarding at the public pool.
  - ▷ Competition for results is anything that absorbs the money or mindshare of your customers, such as alternative dessert options in the local area or online delivery services.

- If you manage a small team in a big company,
  - ▷ Competition for people is anything that attracts your employees to another team or project. It may be a cool new team hiring for similar skill sets in the same company, or it could be another company altogether.

▷ Competition for results is anything that attracts your desired outcome, which may be sales quotas, client satisfaction scores, or online clicks.

Something is constantly trying to out-attract you. Someone wants the attention of your people and their resources. Differentiate between what is competing for your people and what is competing for your results, since it is often not the same thing. Analyzing relative attraction in each area is the best place to start when putting Leadership by Attraction into action.

RELATIVE ATTRACTION ASSESSMENT

People	**Competition:** *Who hires or needs people with skills similar to those you want/need? Who else competes for your target person's time and talents?* P1) .... P2) .... P3) ....
Results	**Competition:** *Who offers similar products or services? Who desires outcomes similar to yours?* R1) .... R2) .... R3) ....

Now let's use our five principles to analyze your competition: Why are they your competition? In what areas is your competition more attractive?

Compare your attraction to each competitor's by judging "you versus them" in each Leadership by Attraction principle. Circle "You" if you are better at attracting than your competition in that principle. Circle "Competition" if you feel out-attracted.

For example, in the first row of Make It Clear's "Who You Are," circle Competition if you feel the competition has clearer, and thus more attractive, values, capabilities, and first response. Are they telling the story of Who They Are better than you are telling the story of Who You Are? You will be basing this answer on how you perceive your competition, your honest opinion of the competition - and isn't that the only measure anyone has? Are they known for fun, or for innovation, or for helping mankind? Are they gaining market share - and specifically why? If you out-attract your competition in every area, reconsider who you consider your competition.

MAKE IT CLEAR		P1		P2		P3		R1		R2		R3	
1	Who You Are	You Competition		You Competition		You Competition		You Competition		You Competition		You Competition	
2	Where You're Going	You Competition		You Competition		You Competition		You Competition		You Competition		You Competition	
	One thing that helps the competition attract here:												

MAKE IT FUN		P1		P2		P3		R1		R2		R3	
1	Celebrating the Journey	You Competition		You Competition		You Competition		You Competition		You Competition		You Competition	
2	Leader's Impact	You Competition		You Competition		You Competition		You Competition		You Competition		You Competition	
3	Obvious Relevant, Fun	You Competition		You Competition		You Competition		You Competition		You Competition		You Competition	
4	Environment/ Atmosphere	You Competition		You Competition		You Competition		You Competition		You Competition		You Competition	
	One thing that helps the competition attract here:												

MAKE IT YOURS	P1	P2	P3	R1	R2	R3
1 Authenticity	You / Competition	You / Competition	You / Competition	You / Competition	You / Competition	You / Competition
2 Vision	You / Competition	You / Competition	You / Competition	You / Competition	You / Competition	You / Competition
One thing that helps the competition attract here:						

MAKE IT THEIRS	P1	P2	P3	R1	R2	R3
1 Ownership	You / Competition	You / Competition	You / Competition	You / Competition	You / Competition	You / Competition
2 Personalization	You / Competition	You / Competition	You / Competition	You / Competition	You / Competition	You / Competition
One thing that helps the competition attract here:						

MAKE IT HAPPEN	P1	P2	P3	R1	R2	R3
1 Speed	You / Competition	You / Competition	You / Competition	You / Competition	You / Competition	You / Competition
2 Quality	You / Competition	You / Competition	You / Competition	You / Competition	You / Competition	You / Competition
One thing that helps the competition attract here:						

Make It Clear:
- Total YOU circled: _____
- Total COMPETITION circled: _____

Make It Fun
- Total YOU circled: _____
- Total COMPETITION circled: _____

Make It Yours
- Total YOU circled: _____
- Total COMPETITION circled: _____

Make It Theirs
- Total YOU circled: _____
- Total COMPETITION circled: _____

Make It Happen:
- Total YOU circled: _____
- Total COMPETITION circled: _____

What are your two *most* attractive principles (where YOU is circled most)?

1. _____

2. _____

What are your two *least* attractive principles (where COMPETITION is circled most)?

1. _____

2. _____

People Competition #1:
- Total YOU circled: _____
- Total THEM circled: _____

People Competition #2:
- Total YOU circled: _____
- Total THEM circled: _____

People Competition #3:
- Total YOU circled: _____
- Total THEM circled: _____

Who is the competition most attractive to your desired PEOPLE?
- #1 or #2 or #3: _____
- What makes them so attractive is: _____

_____

Results Competition #1:
- Total YOU circled: _____
- Total THEM circled: _____

Results Competition #2:
- Total YOU circled: _____
- Total THEM circled: _____

Results Competition #3:
- Total YOU circled: _____
- Total THEM circled: _____

Who is the competition most attractive to your desired RESULTS?

- #1 or #2 or #3: _____
- What makes them so attractive is: _____

_____

PASS **YOUR PIGS**

Pigs are the things, habits, and activities that repel the people and results you want. They gobble up your time and attention, snorting loudly to take your eyes off the prize. Some pigs are covered in lipstick, masquerading as something treasured by you or your team. Pigs make you less attractive as a leader!

Pigs also keep you from Making It Happen. If there's something you wish was happening that isn't, you've got a pig.

You chose to read a leadership book, which means you're probably already successful in many ways and recognize that you could be even more successful. Somewhere in your project or your style, a pig is keeping you from achieving greater success. Pigs aren't always huge. They aren't all prized hogs breaking out to chase little kids on a house showing. Small pigs can make a big mess!

Identifying your pigs is critical because then you can start to pass them.

Root Out Your Pigs

- What's something you wish was happening? _____

    _____

- How important is this thing (1–10)? _____

- What makes it important? _____

    _____

- Which pig(s) might be getting in the way? _____

    _____

Make It Clear: The Ping-Pong Pig

PING-PONG PIG

- Hangs around those who say,
  - ▷ "I can't do one more thing!"
  - ▷ "I'm working as hard as I can!"
  - ▷ "I need my to-do list!"

- Crimes:
  - ▷ Distracting from what matters
  - ▷ Masquerading as important
  - ▷ Squealing for attention

When the urgent and necessary overtake the strategic and intentional.

Think about all the things that fill your days: meetings, phone calls, emails, projects, conversations, brainstorming, and more. What's the reason for doing these things? How do these things contribute to the achievement of your goals?

Anything unimportant is a distraction, a pig that distracts you from Making It Clear. But knowing the difference between what's important, and what's not, is not as easy as it sounds. Being intentional and critical about what steals your time will help you reach clarity.

Take this worksheet for a "ride along" one day this week, and mark the activities that you do each hour. Mark an "X" only when something is Urgent, Necessary, or Strategic. Then, take fifteen seconds to jot down why.

- Urgent—Seems to require immediate action; pressing
- Necessary—Pertains to the steps necessary to remain successful (obtain today's results)
- Strategic—Moves toward the bigger goal (increase tomorrow's results)

WHAT DID I DO?		Urgent?	Necessary?	Strategic?	Why?
	6-7 a.m.				
	7-8 a.m.				
	8-9 a.m.				
	9-10 a.m.				
	10-11 a.m.				
	11-12 p.m.				
	12-1 p.m.				
	1-2 p.m.				
	2-3 p.m.				
	3-4 p.m.				
	4-5 p.m.				
	5-6 p.m.				
	6-7 p.m.				
	7-8 p.m.				
	8-9 p.m.				
	9-10 p.m.				

Total your X's:

- Total Blank: _____
- Total Urgent: _____
  - ▷ Total Urgent & Necessary: _____
  - ▷ Total Urgent & Strategic: _____
- Total Necessary: _____
  - ▷ Total Necessary & Strategic: _____
- Total Strategic: _____

Blank

Examine blanks closely. Why are you spending time on anything that is not Urgent, Necessary, or Strategic? These time sucks are distractions from what you should be doing.

Urgent and Necessary

This could be a symptom of poor planning. If it's truly necessary to your business or project, it should not come as a surprise. At the very least, make sure to learn lessons from your Urgent and Necessary things; you'll likely be able to avoid unexpected urgency next time.

Urgent and Strategic

If you've marked more than three things as Urgent and Strategic, you're not being honest. Daily activities should not be both truly urgent *and* truly strategic. If your reaction to this paragraph is that you really do have many urgent and strategic things, I bet you don't have clarity on what's truly strategic.

Necessary and Strategic

This is where everyone argues. This is where people are stuck doing essential tasks, thinking they are strategic. Routine tasks that keep the business operating are important, but they do not move things toward the bigger goal. They may permit success today, which can seem strategic, but they are not growth oriented and future focused.

Remember, you've only mapped out one day. How typical was this day? Here's the goal: every 14 days you should be able to look back and spot/name the strategic activities that moved your business forward. Any longer review (like every 30 days) means a slower pace to Make It Happen.

You Have a Ping-Pong Pig If:

- > 1 thing is Blank
- > 3 things are Urgent and Strategic
- > 3 things are Necessary and Strategic
- < 1 thing is marked only as Strategic

Pass the Ping-Pong Pig

Determining what's most important can be the most challenging of all of the pig problems. Once you do that, you must make a serious, unbreakable commitment to taking action on that thing every single day. There will always be other things to do, but determine your day's success or failure based on your ability to make progress toward whatever is most important for *your time.*

If you are truly stuck with a Ping-Pong Pig, deciding what's most important may make you irritable and frustrated—the "it's impossible" response. If that's you, this activity may help. Remember, you're after clarity.

CONFIDENCE IN CRITERIA

To build clarity on what's most important, establish criteria to help. You can use these criteria to weigh the options and hone in on what's truly most important.

CLARITY CRITERIA BANK

Example criteria include:

- Urgency
- Revenue generated
- Confidence in executing
- Enjoyment in executing
- Impact on other activities/needed tasks
- What happens if it doesn't happen
- Who is impacted if it doesn't happen
- Possibility of delegating effectively
- Joy, relief in completion

Creating criteria for what's most important builds confidence in knowing what matters. Once you know what matters, you can identify small steps to take each day or each week. Remember, the gap between taking a step and seeing results frustrates everyone—so make each step toward the big vision clear.

1. First, separate urgent and important in your mind and accept that they are not the same thing. Make sure you've completed the previous exercise.

2. List on a piece of paper the criteria that help you judge what's most important. Use the "Clarity Criteria Bank" for thought starters.

3. Rank your criteria from most important to least important.

4. Imagine that you can do the activities that meet Criterion 1, but nothing else. How does that feel? Are you crying because you really need to meet Criterion 2?

5. Reorder as needed based on only meeting Criterion 1.

6. Imagine that you can do activities that meet Criteria 1 and 2, but nothing else.

7. Reorder as needed based on only meeting Criteria 1 and 2.

8. Stop. You could keep going, but you probably already have the two criteria most important to creating Clarity.

Use the carefully prioritized (and often reprioritized) list of criteria, to find clarity on one or two activities that are most important.

Make It Fun: The Party-Pooper Pig

PARTY-POOPER PIG

- Hangs around those who say,
  - ▷ "Happy Friday."
  - ▷ "As soon as this class is over, I'll go have fun."
  - ▷ "If we need to have fun, just plan a happy hour."
  - ▷ "I just can't go through one more boring day here."

- Crimes:
  - ▷ Draining energy with numbing routine
  - ▷ Trudging and slogging through the days
  - ▷ Planning irrelevant fun that takes away from personal time

When energy and buzz become toil and drudgery.

Are you energized by what you're doing? Make It Fun is all about creating that attractive buzz and energy. Party-Pooper Pig brings toiling, which makes for humdrum, boring, unenthusiastic days that chip away at people and results.

How long are you going between energizers? Look back at your calendar and answer these questions with specific dates and events.

Celebrate the Journey

- When's the LAST time you were excited to come into work?

  _____

- When's the NEXT time you'll be excited to come into work?

  _____

- How many days between? _____

Consider Your Impact

- When's the LAST time you energized others?

  _____

- When's the NEXT time you will energize others?

  _____

- How many days between? _____

Make It Obvious

- When's the LAST time you made something fun also relevant, or something relevant also fun?

  _____

- When's the NEXT time you will make something fun also relevant; or relevant also fun?

  _____

- How many days between? _____

Environment

- When's the LAST time you got together with others and learned from them?

  _____

- When's the NEXT time you will get together with others and learn from them?

  _____

- How many days between? _____

Why Does the Gap Matter?

Make It Fun is all about energy, and energy is consumed over time. So, replenishing energy on a regular basis is critical. Fun things that have become routine might be losing their fun or relevance, making this a tricky gap to analyze. Usually though, the warning signs are a lack of analysis, a belief that fun doesn't matter, or the unfounded belief that it can't be driven from the top-down. Without intentionality behind Make It Fun, you're heading for a Party-Pooper Pig.

You Have a Party-Pooper Pig if:

- > 60 days pass between any of these situations (or you've never done it)

Pass the Party-Pooper Pig

Party-Pooper Pig comes out for many reasons including contentment, boredom, and exhaustion. Sometimes this pig is just a lack of attention or a lack of belief that efforts will actually matter. Leaning into one piece of Leadership by Attraction can help boost another. So, if your tank is too empty to have any fun, to look forward to anything, or to see relevance in activities outside of day-to-day work, it may be time to Make It Yours, while also Making It Fun.

What do you enjoy? What sparks joy? Bring that hobby, passion, or interest into your workday and share it with those around you. It can start small and simple to build energy.

Here are a few micro-experiments you could try:

- Listen to a new playlist on your commute, and then share it with your team or colleague

- Read an article, or watch a TED Talk, and discuss it with a coworker

- Start a meeting by going around the room answering: "When surfing the web, what can you not help but click and read?"

The point of focusing on Make It Fun is to focus on wrangling your Party-Pooper Pig. By sharing something you find interesting, there's a good chance you'll feel new energy and see a path to more relevant fun. Sharing and connecting with others encourages others to help increase the energy too.

Make It Yours: The Parked Pig

PARKED PIG

- Hangs around those who say,
  - ▷ "I don't care anymore."
  - ▷ "I just want my paycheck."
  - ▷ "I'm counting down to the day I can leave."

- Crimes:
  - ▷ Stagnation
  - ▷ Apathetic contentment
  - ▷ Just occupying a position or title, not mattering to the role
  - ▷ Too much daydreaming without doing

When passion and purpose become distant.

If you don't care, you are not attractive. This is not harsh criticism. It's fine to not care, but it won't draw people to you and drive your results. Maybe you don't realize that you've stopped caring or you can't muster the courage to move on to what's next.

Since you must care to be an attractive leader, the pig for Make It Yours is not caring enough to bring your authentic self, create a big vision, and/or continue your individual growth. Some need this short quiz to recognize distance from their leadership role. Others look at this page and instantly realize, "I just have a job." A leader with a mission, a passion, or a purpose is more attractive than a leader who just has a job. You might not feel the lack of people or results yet, but when a job is just a job, you're not attracting as much success as you could be.

Rate how much you associate with the following behaviors.

1 - This is not at all like you

4 - This is exactly like you

	1	2	3	4
I leave work energized about my day.				
I feel appreciated by those around me.				
I am productive most of the time.				
I'm willing to give "above and beyond."				
I use my unique skills, talents, or hobbies.				
I learn new things constantly.				
People know something personal about me.				
I talk about my/our goals.				

You Have a Parked Pig if:

- < 26 points total

Pass the Parked Pig

You're stuck in mediocrity, counting the days to retirement, the weekend, the end of a project, and so on. Depending on the size of your Parked Pig, you may need some serious intentionality to pass it. Lean into Make It Happen because doing the minimum has become the norm and excitement about today's tasks feels distant. That's not who you want to be, so get busy and make something happen. Do not allow yourself to settle for the same old same old in every moment of your day. For some people, change creates stress, but when you're parked, even stress can be a good thing. Go for some change, and do it now.

HOW BIG IS YOUR PIG?

Small Parked Pig? Keep what must be done and change how it's done. Change your routine. Next, find a side project. A little something on the side that reengages your brain power, leadership, time, and energy can spread that energy to other parts of your day. Get momentum from something new, and then apply that to your leadership through scheduling tricks, such as working on your pig immediately after an energy boost from your side project.

Medium Parked Pig? Call in reinforcements. Make relevant connections, discuss the obstacles with others, and look for new ideas that can come from these connections. If necessary, delegate. It may be time to move this responsibility to someone with the energy and drive to do it well. Find something that once took your full engagement that is now less stimulating. Give it to someone who can learn from it, and grow by taking on a difficult new problem or expanding your vision.

Big Parked Pig? Hire a coach—a trained professional, not your spouse or friend. Coaching is a learned skill, and a good coach can change your life. They bring clarity to where you really are and where you really want to go, and then help you create a map for the journey. A coach is not a teacher or a trainer; this is not a knowledge transfer. It's about mapping out next steps to ensure progress toward a goal of your choice and finding the knowledge you need along the way. When you have genuinely checked out—lost interest, desire, drive, or belief—a great coach can make a big difference.

Make It Theirs: The Pile-It-On Pig

PILE-IT-ON PIG

- Hangs around those who say,
  - ▷ "I can do it better."
  - ▷ "I can do it faster."
  - ▷ "I don't have [time, money, resources] to find someone else."

- Crimes:
  - ▷ Territorialism
  - ▷ Overly dominant attitude
  - ▷ Inability to see alternatives
  - ▷ Fear

When delegation and trust are stuck.

Most people get that a leader who hordes responsibility and does it all will repel good people. But can you see how that same leader will repel good results? If you do it all, you are not attractive and the reason you do it all does not matter.

What's something that needs to be done? Circle all the reasons why it's easier if *you* do it:

- I'm too busy to teach someone.
- I'm too tired to show someone.
- I can do it better.
- This is my thing.
- It's too important.
- I've always done this.
- I don't know what I'll do if I don't.

- I don't have anyone who can.
- They're going to make mistakes.
- I have the wrong talent around me.
- I don't know how to recruit the right talent.
- I don't know how to develop the right talent.

Leaders are consumed with problem solving. Something needs to get done, and you need to solve a problem to get it done. In fact, problem solving is likely the very thing that has helped you succeed.

What's beneath the surface of these problems? There's a reason leaders solve these problems themselves, and it's often an excuse for not knowing *how* to give that problem away. Leading through others is a skill not typically developed until it's needed. You fall back on solving problems yourself rather than investing in the growth of others—until you learn another way—even when you know others' growth is the secret to your own growth.

Think about your problem as an iceberg. If you could solve it, you wouldn't have circled any surface-level statements. If you knew how to Make It Theirs quickly, easily, and effectively, you would happily give away the responsibility. All surface-level statements are rooted in what's below the surface.

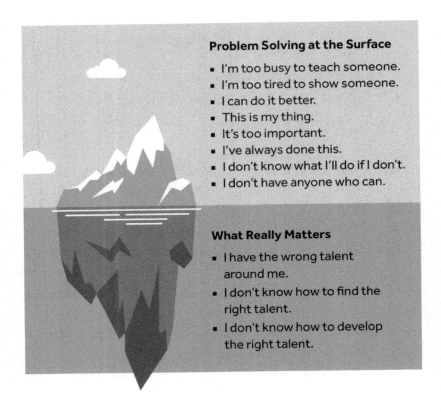

Problem Solving at the Surface

- I'm too busy to teach someone.
- I'm too tired to show someone.
- I can do it better.
- This is my thing.
- It's too important.
- I've always done this.
- I don't know what I'll do if I don't.
- I don't have anyone who can.

What Really Matters

- I have the wrong talent around me.
- I don't know how to find the right talent.
- I don't know how to develop the right talent.

You Have a Pile-It-On Pig If:

- \> 2 statements above the surface are circled

Make It Theirs: Pass the Pile-It-On Pig

You cannot do it all. Theoretically everyone knows not to even try; a great team will go further. But things get busy, and too often it's just too easy to do it yourself. That's when you get exhausted and start dropping some of the balls you're juggling. Suddenly, you hit the achievement ceiling, a barrier to getting anything else accomplished.

Your talent and ambition to do as much as you possibly can are blocking your success.

Ask: "Am I doing it the best I can do it—or the best it can be done?" You want things done the best they can be done, so be honest about where it could be done better. Chunk down big tasks into smaller ones to figure out which ones can be done better by someone else. Get serious about what you can delegate.

The next question for passing this pig is "Who can help me?" It can be a little help or a lot of help. It can be short-term, "right now" help or long-term, committed help. It can be someone doing you a favor or a new hire.

To think like someone who's passed the Pile-It-On Pig entirely, ask, "*Should* I be doing this?" Sometimes you can hire help for fewer dollars per hour than you currently earn, doing the activity yourself doesn't even make financial sense.

It's funny how pigs circle around each other. The most important question is not "How can I do it all?" You know you can't. Instead, it's "How can I do what's most important?"

Saying yes to everything means saying no to what's most important. You simply cannot do it all. Revisit how to pass the Ping-Pong-Pig to stay focused on the most important things and quit piling it on.

STAY CONNECTED TO
LEADERSHIP BY ATTRACTION

When I first started making presentations in my leadership roles, I stuffed them chock full of facts that I could spew at the audience. People needed umbrellas to protect themselves from my barrage! I truly believed I was motivating. I was "helping," after all, by shoving them into action. Now I realize that I was just talking at them and not leading them to a true aha moment or epiphany in which they learned something for themselves!

As my leadership journey continued, I noticed that my impromptu moments—when I'd just pull up a stool and talk—had more impact than my fact spewing. It was more genuine engagement, with some content, some information, and some inspiration, all mixed with me being me. That really mattered.

Now I wake up trying to Make It Clear, Make It Fun, Make It Yours, Make It Theirs, and Make It Happen… but my days are not pig-free. I forget. I get busy. I get overwhelmed and lost and distracted. Finding ways to refocus, reenergize, and continue learning is critical to growing my Leadership by Attraction. I do that by connecting with others and finding information and inspiration to help me add genuine value to those I've attracted and who've attracted me.

I need community to stay dynamic, vital, valuable, and optimistic, and finding people on a similar mission isn't always easy.

LeadershipByAttraction.com connects others working toward the goal of being attractive, significant leaders for families, charities, industries, teams, and businesses. Here we can build a community of leaders increasing their attraction to achieve bold missions and spread personal hope.

If you enjoyed this book—if you spotted a pig or saw a way to better attract your people and thus your results—I want to hear from you.

So, Make It Happen and fight off the pigs. I'll see you there.

AFTERWORD

Writing this book has been a group project, and a commitment. First, I need to say thank you to my son, Jeff, who has been my coach and co-author through this long process. He is such a talented writer himself, and a dedicated coach who willingly accepted the challenge of getting this project, and me, to the finish line. Having Jeff in my world makes my world a better place every single day.

Second, how can I ever thank my husband Mike who is my biggest champion, my lifelong supporter and the one who allows me to be strong. We have always said that you should strive to marry someone who makes you better – and Mike does that for me in every way, every day, no matter what. It's been a wild ride, full of shared adventures and he is always "all in" for whatever is next!

My son Patrick inspires me to remain committed, to pursue the dream, to believe I can make a difference. A special shout out to my in-laws, AJ and Amanda, who willingly and knowingly chose to join our family. A family who is always busy with projects, working on some big vision. They let us share in their own dreams and plans, and they have jumped in to love and support, no matter which path is ahead of us at the moment.

Finally, through the years, I have had friends that know the real me, and somehow, they love me anyway. To my high school friend Kay who wore her T-shirt right along with me that said : "A woman's place is in the House...and the Senate." My college friends continue to provide a safe place, a group of strong intelligent women that are so full of love and fun. My Flower Mound friends loved me through my contentious political years, when being my friend some days put them in the "line of fire" too. The MOB (Mothers of Boys) helped each other be strong and sane while raising future leaders. My friend Annette has lived through most of these stories with me, and I literally would not be me without her love and friendship!

Thank you to Darryl Chauvin in LaPlace, Louisiana who gave me my first shot as an officer of a business, my first opportunity as a sales person and business development specialist. Thanks for letting my creativity and drive run free!

To my RE/MAX friends who introduced me to the world of real estate, and who opened so many doors for me. To my Keller Williams friends who supported me as I grew in both leadership and coaching. To Linda and Jimmy McKissack who showed me the power of an expanding horizon and the art of the possible. To Anna McKissack who is one of the smartest and strongest young leaders I know, who encouraged me and pushed me at a time when it would have been too easy to operate on automatic. To my first coach John Prescott who had the patience to show me that accountability was not something done to you, but something that was for you. A special shout out to Claire Garlick and Colleen Kelley for their time in giving me genuine feedback and suggestions. A very special thank you to David Osborn for teaching abundance, for the inspiration and encouragement in writing, and for believing in my leadership. And to Smokey Garrett, for approaching each day with dogged determination and constantly showing those in his world the power of Hope and A Step.

I wish that my Dad was here with me, but I know he can see this book. He was the one who demonstrated daily that it was possible to be a business success and also let your faith shine through in everything you do. In our house, you were expected to be all that you could be. You were expected to lead, not just join.

My love & thanks to my nieces and nephews who are part of the motivation for creating a book like this - strong, smart, loving individuals who have the power to change the world. A special shout out to Christie and Lauren who were willing to jump in and help along the way.

And finally to George Getschow who convinced me to Run with The Pigs!

I am full of gratitude, joy, love and anticipation. Thank You are two such small words to carry such big emotions.

Made in USA - North Chelmsford, MA
1239793_9781641846011
02.25.2021 1235